THE SEARCH FOR ABRAXAS

ALSO BY NEVILL DRURY

The Varieties of Magical Experience: Indigenous, Medieval and Modern Magic (with Lynne Hume, Praeger, 2013)

Dark Spirits: The Magical Art of Rosaleen Norton and Austin Osman Spare (Salamander, 2012)

Pathways in Modern Western Magic (as editor, Concrescent, 2012)

Stealing Fire from Heaven: The Rise of Modern Western Magic (OUP, 2011)

The Magic of Pan: Rosaleen Norton and the Western Esoteric Tradition, PhD thesis (VDM Verlag/Lambert Academic, 2011)

Homage to Pan: The Life, Art and Sex Magic of Rosaleen Norton (Creation Oneiros, 2009)

The Watkins Dictionary of Magic (Watkins, 2005)

The New Age: The History of a Movement (Thames & Hudson, 2004)

Magic and Witchcraft: From Shamanism to the Technopagans (Thames & Hudson, 2003)

Sacred Encounters: Shamanism and Magical Journeys of the Spirit (Watkins, 2003)

The Dictionary of the Esoteric (Watkins, 2002)

The History of Magic in the Modern Age (Constable, 2000)

Exploring the Labyrinth: Making Sense of the New Spirituality (Continuum, 1999; Allen & Unwin, 1999; Gill & Macmillan.

The Visionary Human: Mystical Consciousness and Paranormal Perspectives (Prism, 1998)

Echoes from the Void: Writings on Magic, Visionary Art and the New Consciousness (Prism, 1994)

The Shaman and the Magician: Journeys Between the Worlds (Arkana, Penguin, 1988)

Pan's Daughter: The Magical World of Rosaleen Norton (Collins Australia, 1988; rpt. as *The Witch of Kings Cross*, Kingsclear Books, 2002; Mandrake, 2013)

Dictionary of Mysticism and the Occult (Harper & Row, 1985, Droemer Knaur, 1988)

Other Temples, Other Gods: The Occult in Australia (with Gregory Tillett, Methuen, 1980)

Inner Visions: Explorations in Magical Consciousness (RKP, 1979)

The Occult Sourcebook (with Gregory Tillett, RKP, 1978)

Don Juan, Mescalito and Modern Magic: Mythology of Inner Space (RKP, 1978)

The Path of the Chameleon: Encounter with the Gods and Magic (Spearman, 1973)

ALSO BY STEPHEN SKINNER

Advanced Flying Star Feng Shui (Golden Hoard, Llewellyn, 2015)

Techniques of Solomonic Magic (Golden Hoard, Llewellyn, 2015)

Techniques of Graeco-Egyptian Magic (Golden Hoard, Llewellyn, 2014)

Key to the Latin of Dr John Dee's Spiritual Diaries (Golden Hoard, Llewellyn, 2012)

Feng Shui History: the Story of Classical Feng Shui in China & the West (GHP, 2012)

Dr John Dee's Spiritual Diaries: the fully revised edition of 'A True & Faithful Relation of what passed ... between Dr John Dee ... & some Spirits' (Golden Hoard, 2011)

Geomancy in Theory & Practice (Golden Hoard, Llewellyn, 2011)

Sepher Raziel: Liber Salomonis (with Don Karr, Golden Hoard, 2010)

The Veritable Key of Solomon (with David Rankine, Golden Hoard, Llewellyn, 2010)

Sepher Raziel: Liber Salomonis (with Don Karr, Golden Hoard, Llewellyn, 2010)

The Grimoire of Saint Cyprian: Clavis Inferni (with David Rankine, Golden Hoard, 2009)

Guide to the Feng Shui Compass (Golden Hoard, 2008)

The Goetia of Dr Rudd: Liber Malorum Spirituum (with David Rankine, Golden Hoard, 2007)

The Complete Magician's Tables (Golden Hoard, Llewellyn, 2006, 2015)

Sacred Geometry: Deciphering the Code (Gaia, 2006; Hamlyn, 2006; Sterling, 2006)

The Water Dragon (with Chang Ping Lin, Golden Hoard, 2006; CreateSpace 2016)

The Keys to the Gateway of Magic (with David Rankine, Golden Hoard, 2005)

Keys to the Gateway of Magic (with David Rankine, Golden Hoard, 2005)

The Practical Angel Magic of Dee's Enochian Tables (with David Rankine, Golden Hoard, 2004)

Feng Shui Style (Periplus, 2004; Tuttle, 2009)

K.I.S.S. Guide to Feng Shui (Keep it Simple Series) (Penguin, DK, 2001)

Feng Shui the Traditional Oriental Way (Parragon, 1997, 1998, 1999, 2002; Diane 1997)

Millennium Prophecies: Apocalypse 2000 (Carlton, 1994)

Nostradamus (with Francis King, Carlton, 1993)

Terrestrial Astrology: Divination by Geomancy (Routledge, 1980)

Oracle of Geomancy (Warner Destiny, 1977; Prism, 1987)

Techniques of High Magic: A Manual of Self Initiation (with Francis King, C.W. Daniel, 1976; Affinity, 1997; Inner Traditions, 2000; CreateSpace, 2016)

Living Earth Manual of Feng Shui (RKP, Penguin, Arkana, 1976, 1981, 1991, 2006)

3

Figure 1: An authentic Gnostic Abraxas talisman.

The Search for Abraxas

by Nevill Drury & Stephen Skinner

Introduction by Colin Wilson

GOLDEN HOARD
2016

First published in Great Britain in 1972 by Neville Spearman Limited
Second English edition published 2013 by Salamander & Sons
Third Edition published 2016 by CreateSpace/Golden Hoard Press

Golden Hoard Press
P O Box 1073 Robinson Road
Singapore 902123

www.GoldenHoard.com

www.SSkinner.com & NevillDrury.com

ISBN: 978-0-9932042-4-1

Figure 2: Ink drawing of Abraxas by Nevill Drury, based on antique Gnostic talismans.

"Our god is named Abraxas and he is both god and the devil at the same time. You will find in him both the world of light and of shadows. Abraxas is not opposed to any of your thoughts or to any of your dreams but he will abandon you if you become normal and unapproachable. He will abandon you and look for another pot in which to cook his thoughts."

— Hermann Hesse

CONTENTS

ILLUSTRATIONS

INTRODUCTION TO THE THIRD EDITION

I have first to record my debt to my co-author, Nevill Drury. We met while we were both doing our Arts degree at Sydney University. It was a time of great excitement, and with the arrival of the 'hippie revolution' and the work of Albert Hoffman, the boundaries of what could be known were vastly expanded. Inner space became even more fascinating than outer space, and I launched and edited one of the new psychedelic magazines, *Chaos,* for which Nevill did much of the artwork. In turn Nevill introduced me to the rock music of that era, and incidentally some very good parties, and I introduced him to the Qabalah and magic. Nevill passed away in October 2013, after an incredibly productive life in the worlds of magic, art and music. He took his Ph.D late in life, and was seminal in persuading me to do the same, something I shall always be grateful to him for. My studies and interests have come a long way since this first tentative investigation of other worlds and the experiences which allowed access to them.

Our identification of Abraxas as a key god was right on target, for my Ph.D studies of the Graeco-Egyptian papyri have confirmed that what was once, 40 years ago, a symbol of transformation for us, now turns out to be one of the most important gods related to magic. It is ironic that more than 40 years after writing *The Search for Abraxas* I returned again to Abraxas, but this time for my Classics Ph.D on the papyri that first mention his name.

The Graeco-Egyptian papyri (*PGM*) are the oldest and most extensive detailed instructions for the practice of magic in the West, dating from the first four centuries AD. They are also the root of much that came later like the grimoires. Egyptian religious records are plentiful, but texts on magic are not. The core of these papyri (the so-called 'Theban library') is a collection of methods and magical techniques made or collected by just one practicing magician.

Although Egypt was always famous for magic, it took Greek genius to organise it into an ordered and (dare I say it) scientific form. Just as the Greek genius Euclid (who lived in Alexandria) systemised the whole world of plane geometry circa 300 BCE, so the Greek speaking magicians responsible for the *PGM* organised magic into 40+ procedures and techniques.

I am pleased to have been instrumental in delineating this system which is laid out in detail in my book on Graeco-Egyptian magic.[1] Prior to my work, the true structure of this magic was hidden from those researchers who relied solely on a range of English translations, by a number of scholars who, failing to value the scientific precision of Greek magical terminology, uniformly translated these many Greek technical words simply as 'spell' or 'charm'. Indeed the English vocabulary for both magic and geometry is pitifully small compared to the detailed and precise vocabulary of the ancient Greeks.

Further to the actual production of this book, as Nevill mentions in his introduction, he offered the idea to the publisher Neville Armstrong. Probably with the objective of getting rid of the eager young author in front of him, Neville Armstrong said that if we could deliver a final manuscript within a month he would accept it for publication. We both liked a challenge, so Nevill returned to Sydney immediately and we started writing. Indeed we did make the deadline (all laboriously handwritten and then typed on a portable typewriter) and airmailed the manuscript back to London.

It is also very satisfying to see that Nevill and I saw the brilliance of Austin Osman Spare's work, both as magic and as art, long before he became a popular resource for works on sigil magic and Chaos magic theory. I went on to publish two of his books, again long before books began to be written about him.[2]

I have taken the liberty of marking which chapters were written by Nevill and which by me, and this indeed became an indication of our later respective career paths: Nevill's in magic, music, shamanism and art, and mine in practical magic, Qabalah, grimoires, Gnosticism and eventually Graeco-Egyptian magic. Three very rough sketches by Austin Osman Spare have been dropped from this edition as they seemed out of place next to his more considered work.

- Stephen Skinner,
Singapore, 2016

---

[1] Stephen Skinner, *Techniques of Graeco-Egyptian Magic*, Singapore, Golden Hoard, 2014.
[2] *Earth: Inferno* and *Focus of Life* first republished by Askin, London, 1976.

INTRODUCTION TO THE SECOND EDITION

More than 40 years have now passed since the release of *The Search for Abraxas* – a book which Stephen Skinner and I both look back on with a certain fondness because it was our first publication. The book obviously reflects some of the predictable weaknesses associated with youthful exuberance – we were both in our mid-twenties when the book was released. However we were unaware until the book was actually in its production phase that the publisher, London-based Neville Spearman, had invited the well known British novelist and occult writer Colin Wilson to contribute an introduction. We were delighted that Wilson described the book as "the manifesto of a new generation" for this was generous praise and we were certainly not expecting it. Wilson concluded with these remarks – "What will spring from it remains to be seen" – and it is certainly true that our commitment to this particular area of research remains ongoing. Stephen and I have both immersed ourselves in esoteric writing and publishing since *The Search for Abraxas* was first released in 1972.The Western magical tradition as a whole continues to fascinate and inspire us.

I think it is true that when one takes that initial step into the Mystery traditions there is no going back, and there are themes hinted at in *The Search for Abraxas* that would become pivotal to both of us in our various lines of research. In my case, I continue to be fascinated by the connection between magical thought and visionary art – whether we are talking about the potent states of magical consciousness explored by such artists as Austin Osman Spare or Rosaleen Norton, or the more mythic forms of visionary art produced by Surrealists like Max Ernst, Wifredo Lam and Wolfgang Paalen. I also have an ongoing personal interest in shamanism, trance states, paranormal experiences, and the history of the Western magical tradition, and have retained my love for publications associated with the Golden Age of British book illustration – especially work featuring such artists as Edmund Dulac, Arthur Rackham, Harry Clarke, S. H. Sime, and Willy Pogany.

Some of the images reproduced in the present volume reflect that ongoing interest.

Following publication of *The Search for Abraxas,* Stephen branched off into numerous other esoteric activities including specialised work on geomancy, Crowleyan *Thelema* and practical magic, in due course co-authoring a major publication with Francis King titled *Techniques of High Magic* and editing various works by Aleister Crowley. Turning his attention to the Orient, he also produced several books on *feng-shui* – he was the first person to write on this subject for a Western audience – and he became one of the first publishers to specialise in producing quality facsimile reprints of important magical texts, like Dr. Meric Casaubon's 1659 edition of Dr. John Dee's spiritual diaries and Henry Cornelius Agrippa's *Fourth Book of Occult Philosophy.* He also issued facsimile editions of Austin Spare's *Earth: Inferno* and *The Focus of Life* through his Askin Publishers imprint, and this specialised work is still continuing with his Golden Hoard imprint. So for both of us *The Search for Abraxas* was very much a catalyst leading to other things, a key point of departure enabling us to explore related areas of magical research in greater depth.

The way in which *The Search for Abraxas* came about may be of interest to readers of this new edition. Stephen and I first met each other at Sydney University in 1968 and indeed it was he who first introduced me to the study of the Qabalah, a subject which has inspired me ever since. In 1970, while working as a school teacher in rural New South Wales, I happened upon the first edition of a new part-work publication titled *Man, Myth and Magic* and was immediately struck by its dramatic cover image which featured a painting of a supernatural entity by Austin Spare. Keen to find out more about this unfamiliar visionary artist I decided to research his background. At this stage there was no substantial information on him of any kind, with the exception of a very brief essay by Kenneth and Steffi Grant, published in 1961 as one of the *Carfax Monographs.*[1] In 1971, while based in London, I obtained a reader's ticket to the British Museum and was able to read Spare's self-published books first-hand.

As a young man Spare had won a scholarship to the Royal College of Art but his brilliant skills as a figurative artist would soon be overshadowed

---

[1] The ten *Carfax Monograph* essays, which also profiled Aleister Crowley and the Hermetic Order of the Golden Dawn as well as describing the Kabbalistic Tree of Life, Frater Achad's 'cosmic snowflake' and the Witches' Sabbath, would later be reissued as *Hidden Lore* in a limited edition of 1,000 copies (Skoob Publishing, London, 1989).

by his eccentric exploration of visionary trance states, sorcery and sigil magic. Publications like *Earth: Inferno* (1905), *A Book of Satyrs* (1907) and his master-work, *The Book of Pleasure (Self-Love):The Psychology of Ecstasy* (1909-1913) were clearly not the work of a conventional artist and it was understandable, while also very regrettable, that his creative genius had not been acknowledged in any of the major British art histories.

Excited by the scope of Spare's vision, I decided to seek out London publishers who might be interested in his art and ideas, and I eventually found my way to the office of occult publisher Neville Spearman Armstrong in Whitfield Street, not far from the Museum. At the time the imprint of Neville Spearman was associated with well known occult writers like Francis King, Trevor Ravenscroft and Erika Cheetham and its publications were wide-ranging in scope, covering such subjects as modern Western magic, the prophecies of Nostradamus, paranormal research, and alchemy. I wasn't really surprised that Neville Armstrong quickly warmed to the idea of a book describing the magical imagery of Austin Spare because the artworks themselves were so remarkable, but it was equally clear that such a book would also have to be broader in scope. I returned to Australia and after co-opting Stephen as my co-author we decided together to produce a book that would explore some of the major themes in the Western esoteric tradition and the philosophies and cosmologies underpinning them.

Colin Wilson has described this book as a 'manifesto' and I suppose in a sense it is – although as far as I can remember we did not start out to produce a tract that was purely polemical. A key element in what we finally came up with relates to the imagery associated with the Gnostic deity Abraxas – a god associated with Time and Eternity, whose symbols are found on many ancient Middle Eastern amulets and talismans. The Swiss psychologist Carl Jung and the German novelist Hermann Hesse – both key inspirational figures widely admired in the international counter-culture that Stephen and I embraced at Sydney University in the late 1960s – had both been fascinated by the idea that the figure of Abraxas appeared to represent the polarities of both good and evil. To this extent, the transcendent Gnostic god was emblematic of the very nature of human potential itself. When we titled our book *The Search for Abraxas* this was very much the focus we had in mind: magic is essentially about altered states of awareness that can lead alternatively towards cosmic transcendence and spiritual integration or towards dark alienation and even evil – and these dimensions are all part of the human equation. Our book is structured in very much the same way: it is divided into 'The World of Light', 'The World of Shadows' and 'The World of Dreams' and concludes with a philosophical overview that addresses 'the search for Abraxas' itself.

As co-authors of this reissued work Stephen and I both hope that new readers will find much that is worthwhile in the pages that follow, despite the fact that in several of its key themes *The Search for Abraxas* has been overtaken by more recent scholarship and research. One thing is clear, however: neither Stephen or I could have had any inkling whatsoever in 1972 – when *The Search for Abraxas* was first published – that Austin Spare would eventually be acknowledged as one of the key figures in the Western magical tradition and one of its most original thinkers, as well as becoming a seminal influence on contemporary Chaos magick. Hopefully our book has contributed to this recognition by providing the first detailed commentary on this important visionary artist.

- Nevill Drury
Milton, NSW,
Australia, 2013

INTRODUCTION TO THE FIRST EDITION

It is difficult to maintain a sense of historical perspective about your own epoch. Too much is happening; there are too many trends and events and intellectual fashions, and you can never be sure which of them will appear important in a hundred years time. But it has been borne in upon me recently that a pretty spectacular change really *has* taken place in the past 10 or 15 years – as total and unexpected as some of the great climatic changes of the Pleistocene. When I was writing my first book, at the age of 23 (in 1955), both Europe and America were in the middle of a phase of 'political consciousness'. Most of the intelligent young people were concerned about the Bomb and germ warfare, and a few were even then concerned about overpopulation and pollution of the environment. They marched to Aldermaston, and signed protests about South Africa, and turned up in Trafalgar Square to boo Sir Oswald Mosley when he made speeches about the necessity for Britain to join Europe in a single economic community.

I felt completely out of it, since politics interested me less than poetry, music and religion. This was not a reasoned attitude; it was purely instinctive. I labelled the problem 'the Bombard effect', after the Frenchman Alain Bombard, who sailed a rubber dinghy across the Atlantic in the early '50s, living entirely on plankton and the juices squeezed from fishes. Half-way across, Bombard made the mistake of going on board a passing ship, and eating a good meal; it almost cost him his life, for when he got back into his dinghy, the meals of plankton and squashed fish made him vomit for days before his stomach readjusted.

This, I felt, was the problem that destroyed Shelley and Novalis and Hölderlin and Van Gogh. They had experienced states of mind in which life suddenly became infinitely interesting, in which a tree became a torch of green flame and a night sky a whirlpool of pure vitality. Then they were asked to return to 'ordinary consciousness' and the boundless mediocrity of our commercial civilisation. No wonder they vomited themselves into a state of mental exhaustion. As to me, I half envied these left-wing protesters and marchers; their stomachs were obviously healthier and

17

stronger than mine. For me, their Marxist slogans were only one degree less nauseating than the Bomb itself.

For the remainder of the 1950s, and well into the '60s, the left-wing novelists, playwrights and critics had it all their own way – Amis, Braine, Doris Lessing, Osborne, Wesker, Logue, Tynan, and the rest. (I am confining myself to England, but most other countries could make up their own lists). They seemed unanswerable: that in a world with so many starving people, so many problems requiring political action, it was the worst kind of irresponsibility to find Dostoyevsky and Hesse more interesting than Brecht and Sholokov. They were never slow to point out that such a preference verged on fascism (although I could never follow the logic of this argument). Oddly enough, the philosophical position of these leftists was often curiously pessimistic. They were inclined to accept Freud's disheartening view of human nature: that culture is man's attempt to compensate for the dark forces of the libido, and that the fundamental striving of life is towards death. When Genet compared society to a brothel for perverts, they cheered; when Ionesco and Beckett said that life was meaningless anyway, they nodded sadly. In a sense, this was logical; for if life is as dreary and meaningless as they seemed to think, then there is nothing more important than achieving a fair distribution of wealth.

All this aggressive left-wingery made life somewhat difficult, both for me and for friends who shared my attitudes, like Bill Hopkins and Stuart Holroyd. Our books got panned by critics, who accused us of obscurantism, neo-fascism, and lack of social responsibility. I once pointed out that even Sartre, that inveterate leftist, makes Mathieu, the hero of *Road to Freedom*, speak about the need for individual 'salvation', whereupon a critic replied that Sartre had intended Mathieu to be an example of a bourgeois weakling …

What precisely happened then? I'm damned if I know. All I know is that I continued to write books, and they ceased to be attacked, and were simply ignored. The tide seemed to be as far out as it possibly could be. Then, round about 1966 or '67, the change began. For example, to the amazement of his English and American publishers, the novels of Hermann Hesse began to sell in huge quantities. He had been dead since 1962, and although he had received the Nobel Prize in 1946, it could be said that he had been half-forgotten since the '30s. His novels about individuals who take to the road in search of 'salvation' were apparently as old-fashioned as Galsworthy and Hergesheimer. When I decided to write about Hesse in *The Outsider* in 1954, all his novels were out of print in English, and I had to read them in the British Museum reading room. After the brief fashionable success of *The Outsider*, Hesse's novels began to be reprinted, and American dons wrote articles about him in academic publications (although their bibliographies never included *The Outsider*); but it was still a mere trickle of interest. Then the trickle became a flood, and Hesse again became a best-seller, as he had been in the '20s in Germany.

What seems to have happened is that the beatnik movement, started in America by Kerouac and Ginsberg as a drop-out revolt against bourgeois respectability and the American Dream, outgrew its original anti-intellectualism – the cult of Charlie Parker, Billie Holiday, James Dean – and began to set up a pantheon of intellectual idols that included figures as disparate as Marcuse and Tolkien. The faces on the Beatles' *Sergeant Pepper* LP include Aleister Crowley, Jung, Poe, and Aldous Huxley. Poe one can understand – the outsider who died of neglect in a society interested only in money. And Aldous Huxley who was the real founder of the psychedelic cult with his 1953 book on mescaline. But Jung, with his obscure German syntax, and Crowley, that Dionysian Kabbalist who was mistakenly labelled a Satanist – how on Earth did they manage to seep into the consciousnesses of the pop enthusiasts? I would as soon have expected to find pictures of Einstein or Musil on the LP jacket.

By the late '60s, it was very clear that the Jung-Crowley combination represented a new current of interest. There had always been a small, specialist market for books on occultism. In the early '50s, Rider and Co. of London republished the magical works of Éliphas Lévi, Muldoon on astral projection, and biographies of Hindu mystics; but the market was always sluggish. Ten years later, in America, University Books republished the books of A. E. Waite, Yeats' associate in the Golden Dawn society, and Montague Summers' treatises on vampires and witchcraft. My old friend August Derleth had kept the works of H. P. Lovecraft in print since his death in 1937, but his customers almost amounted to a Lovecraft Book Club; you couldn't walk into a bookshop and buy them off the shelves. I suspect that the audience for all these books remained about as large as the audience for LP records of train noises. Then, suddenly, it began to grow. Works like Regardie's four volume *Golden Dawn*, which could have been purchased for five quid in 1950, was so much in demand that it became worth £80 a set. Early in 1970, a publisher of part-magazines (i.e.

magazines intended to be collected and eventually bound into volumes) embarked on an apparently rash project, the publication of an alphabetical encyclopaedia of magic and occultism in 11 weekly parts; *Man, Myth and Magic* amazed the publishing trade by becoming the magazine equivalent of a best-seller – so successful that it has now been reprinted in 25 volumes.

But even the publishers of these books and magazines found it difficult to explain the precise nature of this enthusiasm. On the surface, it seemed to be the shallow, fashionable, completely unaccountable interest that creates best-sellers. All you can say is that it often seems to be bound with escapism – the Kon Tiki expedition, Jaques Cousteau's undersea adventures, and so on. This certainly seemed to be the case in 1960, when Gallimard brought out in Paris a curious work called *Le Matin des Magiciens* by Louis Pauwels and Jacques Bergier. The book sold and sold, yet its success was difficult to explain. For this was no closely reasoned work on the paranormal, but a kind of rag-bag resembling Ripley's *Believe It Or Not*. The book swoops from quantum theory to the mythology of Lovecraft, from buried cities in the Brazilian jungle to the suggestion that the Nazis were an occult society. A fascinating book, certainly; but the kind of thing that would enrage any logical positivist because its authors seem to have an attitude of blissful indifference towards questions of proof and verification. The English and American editions, published three years later, had nothing like the same success; but they may have been responsible for starting the occult craze that snowballed during the next seven years.

Readers of Sunday newspapers were inclined to believe that all the talk about witch cults was an invention of journalists. Not that anyone doubted the existence of such cults; everyone knew that the works of the late Gerald Gardner – which purported to describe witch cults already in existence – had led to the formation of dozens of such covens. But the general opinion was that these were either harmless religious organisations, practising pagan Nature worship by the light of the Moon, or excuses for voyeurism and sexual orgies. (Gardner was himself a voyeur).The new interest in Crowley seemed to be merely another expression of the anti-authoritarianism of the young. For Crowley, as he emerges in John Symonds' biography *The Great Beast* seems to be a martyr to the romantic-artistic principle of shocking the bourgeoisie. His life was apparently spent cocking a snook at respectability, and respectability reacted by treating him as the outcast he seemed determined to become.

In fact, this whole notion was mistaken. And this brings me, belatedly, to the subject of the present book, and its two young authors. For what readers of *The Great Beast* could be forgiven for failing to understand was that, exhibitionist or not, Crowley was as dedicated and serious a magician as Einstein was a physicist. He belonged to a tradition that believed wholly in the *objective* efficiency of magic.

I must emphasise this, for readers of this introduction will miss the whole point if they fail to grasp it. We are not talking about Rhine's experiments in extra-sensory perception, or about naked girls copulating with a high priest on an altar. We are talking about a belief that has been discredited for the past three centuries, but which has never ceased to be accepted by a small number of men and women, that certain magical operations can produce a result in Nature – as when the North Berwick witches confessed to causing the storm that almost wrecked the fleet of James VI of Scotland when he was returning from Denmark with his newly married bride. We dismiss this as pure delusion. And no practising magician would deny that it *could* have been pure delusion. *But*, he would insist, there *are* forces in Nature, and in the human mind, which can be called upon through certain magical disciplines, and which could cause such a storm. In fact, the more I study the case of the North Berwick witches, the more I am inclined to doubt my original opinion that they were persecuted innocents. There are now plenty of highly convincing accounts of African rain-makers who can call up a storm through tribal ceremonies, and it strikes me as a real possibility that the North Berwick witches may have discovered how to work the same trick.

There are, nowadays, hundreds of serious students of magic who believe that the magicians of the past were really 'on to something': that is a half-forgotten tradition, as alien to our modes of thinking as Balinese music is to ears accustomed to Western music. Their belief rests on two premises, one more-or-less acceptable to the Western mind, the other totally unacceptable. The acceptable premise is that the human mind is bigger and stranger than any psychologist has ever guessed – although Jung came close to it – and that it possesses unexplored powers. They also believe that there is a purely objective component in magic; that there are 'powers and dominions' in Nature, god-like or demonic forces that can be utilised by the human mind when it has learned to draw upon its hidden powers. This notion is, of course, offensive to the Western intellect, although most religions accept something of the sort. (As I write this, the Bishop of Exeter has just created something of a sensation by recommending that all parishes should possess an exorcist for casting out spirits and demons).

A whole school of young practising magicians has sprung up. They are not sensation-seekers or hippies. They pursue their subject with the same seriousness that they might study electronic engineering or radio astronomy. They attempt to control the mind and discipline the imagination, assuming that such discipline may bring into being higher levels of consciousness that in turn may focus and control powers that are inaccessible to ordinary consciousness. You could say that the basic principle is the feeling that 'everyday consciousness' is like a cloud of gnats, all flying aimlessly, changing direction yet maintaining a general shape and position. Magic begins by assuming that these aimless energies could be channelised and ordered, and that the result might be totally unlike anything you could anticipate from studying the behaviour of a cloud of gnats. No one could judge an orchestra from the sounds it makes while tuning up; yet we commit an analogous mistake about the human mind. Or again, we know that ordinary light consists of a mass of tangled energies like a ball of cotton wool; but when these energies have been untangled and brought into step through a ruby laser, the resulting light has the power to cut through metal.

W. B. Yeats has written in his autobiographies of his membership of the magical society called the Order of the Golden Dawn; and ever since Yeats was acknowledged as the greatest of modern Irish poets, commentators have discussed his 'magical' affiliations as if they were a sign of charming eccentricity, the poet's ability to believe a dozen untrue things before breakfast. What had become clear in the past few years is that this view was mistaken; the Golden Dawn was a genuine magical society, bringing to its own experiments the same seriousness that Lord Rutherford brought to the investigation of crystal structures. Moreover, these younger students of magic have taken up where Mathers and Waite left off. Francis King's *Ritual Magic in England* discusses some of these recent groups, and records their claim that they have actually produced 'results'.

The young authors of this present book regard themselves as serious students of the magical tradition.[1] Both live in Australia. Stephen Skinner, born in 1948 in Sydney, is a graduate from Sydney University who is at present a lecturer in a technical college. Nevill Drury, born in 1947, was born in Hastings, Sussex, and has spent half his life in Australia; he is a graduate of Sydney University, and majored in anthropology and modern history. They seem to have approached 'occultism' from opposite positions. Nevill Drury thinks of himself as basically an artist (hence his interest in Austin Spare – see Section II.) His father is an art lecturer at Perth, and Nevill's coloured ink drawings have been on exhibition in Sydney. He became interested in magic through *Le Matin des Magiciens* and the works of Arthur Machen; he also edited the Australian *UFO Review* from 1966 to 1969. A grandmother was an ardent Steiner-ite, and his father came under the influence of Buddhist thought while serving as an officer in the Second World War.

Stephen Skinner began as a student of psychology; in a letter to me, he commented that he found MacDougall's *Abnormal Psychology* and Sinclair's studies in philosophy inadequate to explain the observed phenomena of the mind. The behaviourist psychology he encountered at university also left him thoroughly dissatisfied, since it "seemed to lose sight of the psyche in a maze of stats and Skinner boxes." The psychological need for more 'nutritious' objects of study led him to works on occultism, and on the Qabalah in particular. This highly complex and precise system of mysticism satisfied the need for logical exactitude, and he came to concentrate on Qabalism. The Qabalah prescribes various practical disciplines for exploring 'astral' realms; it might be described as a form of occult behaviourism. It was at this point that Skinner and Drury met – at university – and Drury was impressed by Skinner's Qabalistic erudition (although, as an artist, he finds the theoretical side of Qabalism less interesting than its symbolic and 'intangible' aspects).

Drury's belief that the artist is a *vehicle for*, not a creator of, his artistic productions, produced a desire to explore methods of charting the hidden sources of inspiration. "The levels of inspiration achieved by different artists seems to me to parallel the stages of consciousness outlined in the Qabalah, and for this reason, one of my main aspirations is to achieve greater rapport with the higher levels of my unconscious." And so

---

[1] I wish to thank Eddie Campbell of the *Evening News* – another dedicated student of occult matters – for drawing my attention to the manuscript of these young writers.

Skinner's need for scientific exactitude and Drury's desire to tap hidden levels of subconscious vitality combine in a common purpose. The first result of their cooperation appears in this far-ranging and highly readable book.

To the casual reader, the result will probably seem as vertiginous – if as absorbing – as *Le Matin des Magiciens*. The discussion moves swiftly from Ballou's *OAHSPE*, a book supposedly written at the dictation of an angel, through sketches of Gnosticism and Qabalistic philosophy, to a number of studies of the borderland between art and occultism – especially in the art of Austin Spare, who fascinates both writers.

What the authors have attempted to do, in the briefest possible space, is to present the basis of their studies, the core of their obsessions. They might have attempted a more massive structure, discussing the Qabalah in detail, and attempting to relate the work of various artists to its 'levels of consciousness'. But at the present stage, such a labour would probably be premature. Instead, they have chosen the intuitive method of presentation, to discuss what deeply interests them, leaving the reader to divine all the connections. In some cases, these connections are clear enough. For example, the description of the experiences of Carlos Castaneda as the pupil of Yaqui Indian 'witch doctor' make clear the connection between the Qabalah, the witch cults of the Middle Ages, and the use of hallucinogenic drugs. Sceptics will argue that such experiences – as soaring through the air – could only be produced by drugs, and prove nothing whatever about the reality of 'other' states of consciousness. Drury and Skinner argue that such experiences allow us to glimpse the active powers of the imagination, and that the realms of consciousness glimpsed by Castaneda are an objective reality that can also be explored by Qabalistic disciplines.

The authors of this book represent a new phenomenon: the serious study of the practice of magic. (Another young writer, David Conway, has presented a more systematic exploration of the methods in *Magic, An Occult Primer*, which again lays central emphasis upon the *training* and control of imagination). It is true that 'occult revivals' seem to have occurred in the last decades of the past three centuries, as a reaction against the current of rationalism. What is so interesting about this latest wave of occultism is it is more sober and rational than any of its predecessors. These practising magicians have decided that there *is*

24

something in magic, something as objective as radio waves. They have set out to investigate it in a spirit in which Yeats' romanticism combines with scientific empiricism. They seem determined to get to the bottom of it, or at least, to go further in understanding it than any of their predecessors have attempted, using the discoveries of anthropology, as epitomised in the work of Eliade and Levi-Strauss, and the insights of Jungian psychology. And this seems to me logical, even predictable. In *Religion and the Rebel*, I pointed out that science began as the study of *distant* phenomena, the stars and planets. Then it moved down to Earth, with physics and chemistry. Later came geology, then biology, then psychology, then the social sciences. At each stage there has been a time-lag before these subjects were regarded as respectable enough to teach in universities; man found it hard to believe that anything so close to him as psychology or sociology could be a real science. With each new science, the focus moves further from the outside Universe, in towards man himself. A century ago, it would have been as impossible to take a scientific attitude towards magic as it was for the Victorians to take a scientific attitude towards sexual perversion. It was a bit too near the bone.

Now, at last, we have some of the necessary tools for analysing 'the facts'. The problem now is to find out precisely what the facts are. What Stephen Skinner and Nevill Drury have done in this book is not to make an anthology of the weird and wonderful, but to state, with a kind of modesty and quiet precision, what they consider the relevant facts to be. It is their manifesto, and the manifesto of a new generation. What will spring from it remains to be seen.

- Colin Wilson,
Gorran Haven, 1972

PROLOGUE

his book is about levels of consciousness, and Western Man's pursuit of the Ultimate Level. There are many doctrines and methods leading to this Reality. We deal here with less familiar Paths leading to that exalted state of Being, which we have designated *Abraxas*, because we find it meaningful. There are many other names we could have chosen.

Section I
The World of Light

"Mystics come from the same country
and recognise one another."

- Saint-Martin

I

MODERN REVIVALS

In 1882 an anonymous book named *OAHSPE, A Kosman Bible* was published in New York. It was subsequently revealed in a letter to the Editor of *The Banner of Light*, a Boston periodical, that its author was a dentist named Dr. John Ballou Newbrough and that the book had been written, mostly in the dark, through the agency of automatic writing. Newbrough claimed indeed that the book was written not by himself but through 'some other intelligence' using him as a vehicle.

His interest in spiritualism was long standing. When he was a boy his father felt obliged to discourage his clairvoyant and clairaudient leanings, and when at college, Newbrough had allowed himself to be mesmerised by a visiting lecturer. Later on, Newbrough discovered that when he sat in circles at séances and calmed his mind, his hands would 'fly off into tantrums' producing messages reading in all directions. So it was that he became interested in researching similar spiritualistic incidents in his own country. After examining over 200 cases of mediumship, he became convinced that spiritualistic phenomena were 'angelic' in nature and he himself began to 'crave for the light of heaven'. By this he meant that he wished to become the vehicle for something spiritually profound, rather than mere scribblings and doodles. Consequently Newbrough decided to 'purify' himself, in order to attract the light. He did this by abstaining from meat, fish, milk, and butter, and by critically repenting of his misdeeds. The method evidently worked for he says: "A new lease of life came to me."

Newbrough now found himself able to see and hear the angels who had formerly revealed their presence only by controlling his fingertips in trance. He was 'instructed' to obtain a typewriter and struggled to master it. For two years nothing very much happened in his angelic discourses. But then:

> "One morning the light struck both my hands on the back, and they went for the typewriter for some fifteen minutes, very rigorously. I was told not to read what was printed, and I had worked myself into such a religious fear of losing this new power that I obeyed reverently. The next morning, also before sunrise, the same power came and wrote (or rather printed). Again I laid the matter away very religiously, saying little about it to anybody. One morning I accidentally (seemed accidental to me) looked out of the window and beheld the line of light that rested on my hands extending

heavenward like a telegraph wire towards the sky. Over my head were three pairs of hands, fully materialised; behind me stood another angel, with her hands on my shoulders. My looking did not disturb the scene; my hands kept right on, printing … printing."

"For fifty weeks this continued, every morning half an hour or so before sunrise, and then it ceased, and I was told to read and publish the book *OAHSPE*. The peculiar drawings in *OAHSPE* were made with pencil in the same way."

OAHSPE, which is one of the most remarkable neo-religious books ever published, is some 900 pages in length. It contains, among other things, details of the skills and qualities of spiritual rulers of Earth during different ages in history, and a map of the lost continent of Pan situated in the Pacific between Australia and South America. It describes also, in very lyrical language, magnificent fiery space-vehicles which angels use for cosmic travel. This was some 70 years before unidentified flying objects were becoming objects of popular discussion.[1]

Less fortunately, perhaps, it contains many religious and mythological 'condemnations'. Osiris, for example, is described as a 'false god' and the modern movements Swedenborgism, Mormonism and Shakerism are all regarded as "attempts at false godheads (having) their origin in the lower heavens." The institutions of Christianity, Buddhism, Brahmanism, and Mohammedanism are described as being inspired by false deities which *OAHSPE* names respectively as: Looeamong, Kabalactes, Ennochissa, and Thoth. However there is no criticism of Jesus as such (his 'real' name is Joshu), Buddha (called in *OAHSPE*, 'Sakaya') nor 'Brahma'. Mohammed is not mentioned.

OAHSPE was only *one* of a number of religious innovations in a period of American and European history that saw the emergence of the scientific method and the shattering of many 'fundamentalist' Christian concepts. When it became clear that the world had not indeed been created in the year 4004 B.C. as Bishop Ussher had declared, and that the seven days of Creation were not literal ones, one reaction in the United States was to produce new, and sometimes incredible, versions of the 'Sacred Truth' as the old one appeared to crumble. Dr. Newbrough's *OAHSPE* was not the

---

[1] See N. Drury, 'Flying Ships in *Oahspe*', article in the *Australian Flying Saucer Review* (UFOIC, Sydney), No. 9, 1966.

only, or by any means the most famous, 'holy' work to arise in these years. We observe the growth of Mormonism, which in many ways parallels *OAHSPE* in its 'angelic' origins; the Jehovah's Witnesses of Charles Russell, who stated that non-adherents of his sect, including 'heathen Christians', would not survive Armageddon; and the Christian Scientists of Mary Baker Eddy, who attempted in a certain way to reconcile Christianity with both science and spiritual healing techniques. And even before *On the Origin of Species* and Lyell's treatises on geology which indicated that the Creation was not instantaneous but a long, gradual process, we see that in the United States there were spasmodic outbursts of religious preaching that the world was soon to end and a new religious age about to dawn.

Harriet Livermore, daughter of a congressman from Massachusetts, expressed her belief that Christ was shortly to begin a 1,000 year reign over the Twelve Tribes of Israel. More famous, perhaps, was William Miller whose millenarian teachings culminated in the modern Seventh Day Adventist sect. He estimated that the end of the world would occur in 1834, and then when this proved incorrect despite the fact that it had been calculated by five independent methods, 1843 was set as the new date. Regrettably, this too was an error. Miller sank into despondency and disbelief, leaving the movement which had caused considerable hysteria and mob excitement and won 50,000 adherents.[1]

Another organisation which has experienced various turns of fortune, faced a great deal of criticism, yet counted some notable followers, including D. H. Lawrence and painters Mondrian and Kandinsky, is the Theosophical Society. Founded in New York in 1875 by the Russian, Madame Blavatsky and Colonel Henry Olcott, this movement attempted not so much to revive Christianity as to fuse into a new teaching the strands of truth common to all the great religions. The name 'Theosophy' means literally 'Divine Wisdom'; the Society's motto was "There is no religion higher than truth."

Madame Blavatsky outlines her ideas most succinctly in her book *The Key to Theosophy* first published in 1889. She says here that one of the chief aims was to "reconcile all religious sects and nations under a common system of

---

[1] The Jehovah's Witnesses similarly calculated a date for the end of the world and the second coming of Christ. Russell first stipulated 1874, then 1914. When Christ did not appear visually His arrival was said to be invisible. For more details on sects with an obsession with end times and Armageddon see Skinner, *Millennium Prophecies,* London, Carlton, 1994.

ethics based on eternal verities." All the world's religions contained a basic truth, asserted Madame Blavatsky, because the "Wisdom Religion was *one* in antiquity."

H. P. B., as she was known to her disciples, personally smoked a pipe, was notably pagan in her religious preferences and believed that she received exclusive sacred messages from a Tibetan 'Master' named Koot Hoomi by means of the postal service. On some occasions she also indulged in trickery during spiritualistic séances in order to prove to her more gullible following that there was adequate proof of the inner realm of Spirit. However, her compendium *The Secret Doctrine* is a vast storehouse of esoteric and mythical lore written in the 1880s when the comparative study of religion was hardly under way. And it is her teachings, rather than her personality quirks, which Theosophists respect and admire most. Few modern avatars, after all, have been perfect.

Theosophy asserts that 'the Truth' is recoverable from a distant historical-mythological past whence it has become obscured, distorted and even forgotten. In effect, Theosophy is not without precedent because the West has always known a tradition of people who claimed special access to the Gnosis (Sacred Knowledge). And the origin of this assertion may indeed trace ultimately right back to the first spark of religious insight in archaic man. Who, then, were the early exponents, in the West, of the 'Sacred Truth' which so many people in such different ways were now trying to re-express?

II

GENESIS OF THE GNOSIS

In the years of cultural flux which saw Christianity arise, the movement known as Gnosticism evolved as an esoteric, heretical shadow, drawing eclectically from traditions that were Egyptian, Hellenistic, Judaic, and Mesopotamian in inspiration. Many Gnostic adherents nevertheless regard themselves as Christian.[1] However there is one crucial difference between the two world views. The Christian waits for an act of Grace from his God; the Gnostic, by contrast, believes that he himself is in control. Through manipulation of sacred names and gematric formulas the invoker beckons the deities to his call. Philo of Alexandria refers to a ladder of words (names) stretching from Heaven to Earth, through knowledge of which man may ascend to God ("In the Beginning was the Word …"). And as Robert M. Grant says: "The Gnostic soul is saved because it knows the secrets of the heavenly spheres and gives the correct answers (i.e. to the deities encountered). From the Hellenistic Gnosis we quote the Mystic Rite of the Flame, wherein man commands his God:

> "Thee I invoke, thou mightiest God and Master… thou who enlightenest all and pourest thy rays by means of thine own power on all the world, O God of gods! … Enter, appear to me, O Lord of mighty names whom all have in their hearts, who dost burst open rocks and mak'st the names of gods to move!"

Irenaeus, who was bishop of Lyons in the late 2nd century, believed it was impossible to control the heavens simply by uttering 'sacred' names. As a Christian he was naturally reticent about the strange gods which seemed to lurk behind the teachings of the Gnostics:

> "They use magic and images and incantations and invocations," wrote Irenaeus, "and after inventing certain names as if they belonged to angels, they proclaim that some are in the first heaven, others in the second, and then try to set forth the names, principalities, angels and powers of the 365 fictitious heavens …"

Who was presumed to be in charge of these heavens? According to Basilides, it was a god named Abraxas, whose name appears engraved upon many Gnostic amulets and talismans (and who also, as a predominant deity of the Gnosis, supplies the title of our book). (See Figure 1 and Figure 2.)

---

[1] "The Gnosis itself is that which has descended by transmission to a few, having been imparted unwritten by the Apostles." Clement of Alexandria, *Miscell.*, Book VI, Ch. 7.

Abraxas had a human body, the head of a hawk and legs of serpents. He was usually shown holding a knife in one hand, and in the other, a shield inscribed with the sacred name JAH. It is believed that in his purest form, Abraxas was a Sun god whose influence over the world extended throughout the year (growth and decline), and cyclically, through all Eternity. The name Abraxas, when equated with numerical values based on the Greek spelling, totals 365, the number of days in a year.[1] For this very reason the superstitious common people engraved their good luck charms with the name Abraxas because they hoped that fortune would then smile upon them from day to day. Abraxas, however, was much more than a daily comforter. He was ruler of the First Heaven, pervader of the seven spheres and Lord of the 365 zones of the inner realm. He was associated with the Creation of the World, and his name, according to Basilides, contained considerable magical power which could make one invincible.

This emphasis upon sacred formulas of power is alien to Christianity, which eventually pronounced Gnosticism to be a heresy. There is, however, much more in Gnosticism that is unusual and heterodox apart from mere formulas. It presents, in fact, a complicated system of mysticism whereby the individual receives inspiration from the Higher Spheres through revelation and then endeavours by his own effort to regain the spiritual heights, either in meditation or in the astral journey of the soul after death. Certain deities of the Lesser Heavens, however, were liable to stand in his way. According to the Ophites, a Gnostic sect, there were seven such obstructive animal demons. Their names were Michael (a lion), Souriel (a bull), Raphael (a hissing snake), Gabriel (an eagle), Ialdabaoth (a lion), Iaoth (a snake), Sabaoth (a bull), Eloaios (an eagle), Thauthabaoth (a bear), Erathaoth (a dog), and Oneol or Thartharoath (an ass). Origen, a Christian theologian writing in the 3rd century, described in his *Contra Celsum* how the Ophites addressed these seven bestial demons on the inner journey. The dialogue ran:

"Hail you, solitary King, Bond of Invisibility, First Power, guarded by the spirit of Foreknowledge and by Wisdom. From this place I am sent on, pure, already a part of the light of Son and Father. Let grace be with me, yes,

---

[1] The numeration of Abraxas in Greek is Alpha-1, Beta-2, Rho-100, Alpha-1, Xi-60, Alpha-1, Sigma-200, totalling 365. In Hebrew the numeration is Aleph-1, Beth-2, Resh-200, Aleph-1, Qoph-100, Aleph-1, Samekh-60, also totalling 365.

Father, let it be with me."

Having conquered the demon with this formula, by appealing to God on high, the soul now proceeded to the more lofty heavens.

In general the Gnostics believed that these heavens (called Aeons or 'eternities' because they were outside space and time) were emanations from a First Principle which might be best visualised as vibrant Energy. The first Aeons were pure and perfect in themselves, but as they reached down closer and closer to the level we call reality, they became tainted by contact with the World. All material things were regarded as basically 'deficient' because they were only dim reflections of the Divine. In fact, because the Earth was created out of chaos, which the Gnostics believed to be devoid of cosmic energy, the 'deficiencies' came to be equated with negativity or evil. Some Gnostics believed also that when the soul fell into matter from its earlier elevated state, it became sorrowful because physical existence involved suffering. And like the Buddha, these Gnostics equated suffering with ignorance. The Path of Self-Knowledge eliminated ignorance and suffering and led to spiritual renewal: Body became Spirit; Evil transmuted itself into Good.

Each Aeon, or emanation from God, is more 'positive' than the one beneath it and correspondingly more real. The Ophite conception is indeed a detailed cosmology of lesser and greater deities. But here we gain an insight into why the Gnostic tradition presented a viewpoint that was antagonistic to Church doctrine in the early centuries. According to the Ophites the First Light came from the Darkness, and He was God the Father, the First Man. His thought gave rise to His Son, the Second Man. A third emanation now arose: the Holy Spirit (Female).[1] Beneath these lay a watery Chaos which saw the birth of the First Woman. The First Man and His Son rejoiced at Her beauty and filled Her with Light, which generated the Third Man, whose name was Christ.[2] The Mother could not sustain the Light, which overflowed on Her left-hand side. Meanwhile Christ, who was on Her right-hand side, ascended in the Light to the level of the First Aeon which placed Him alongside God (the First Man). The overflowing Light now gave rise to seven successive lesser deities: Ialdabaoth, Iao,

---

[1] These three emanations parallel the Supernals, Kether, Chokmah and Binah, in the Qabalah.
[2] The early Fathers of the Christian Church considered Plato's 'Logos' to be identical with their Christos. See J. Stirling, *The Canon, an Exposition of the Pagan Mystery Perpetuated in the Cabala as the Rule of all the Arts*, Elkin Mathews, London, 1897, p. 56.

Sabaoth, Adonai, Elohim, Oreus, and Astapheus, who reigned, in their respective heavens, over things celestial and terrestrial. Christ then descended through these seven heavens into the body of the man Jesus and the latter began both to produce miracles and to preach that he was Christ, Son of God (i.e. Son of the First Man). When Jesus was crucified, Christ departed to the First Aeon but although the body of Jesus perished, Christ provided him with a psychic, spiritual body. It was this, and not a resurrected physical body, that the disciples saw. Thus it was through the teachings and actions of the man Jesus that Christ was able to show humanity the way to the First Aeon, or at least so the Ophites believed. As a system of spiritual redemption the Ophites' viewpoint was bound to be heretical because it bypassed the Church as an authority. It dealt strictly with the direct relationship between man and the First Aeon and the intermediary journey of the soul past the seven animal demons described earlier and the seven lesser spiritual deities named above: it spoke of the final Union with the First Mystery, the Source of Creation – the transcendental God whose name, according to Basilides, was ABRAXAS.

These are the first flowerings of a corporate Gnosis in the West. There were, however, to be further outbreaks of mystical heterodoxy. The 12th and 13th centuries saw the rise in southwest France of the heretical Cathars. They believed in a dualistic Universe where the power of Evil, the demoniac Monster of Chaos, counteracted the omniscience of the Christian God. As a concept it parallels the Gnostic idea of a Universe tainted by the Evil inherent in the Abyss. According to the Cathars, the world and the flesh were basically evil and man's divine spark had to be liberated from the body which engulfed it. These too are Gnostic ideas. More specifically heretical perhaps was the Cathar denial of the Virgin birth, Jesus' death on the Cross, and the physical resurrection. These, they said, were purely fictitious.

Continuing our investigation of the Gnosis we note the alchemystical writings of men like Paracelsus, Thomas Vaughan and Solomon Trismosin, among many others, all of whom presented methods whereby the 'leaden' unenlightened man is transmuted into a state of 'golden' spiritual purity by applying the sacred principles of the Philosopher's Stone: the Great Secret. Incidentally, the 22 alchemical pictures in Trismosin's *Splendor Solis* (1582) have the same allegorical meaning as the 22 Keys of the Tarot, and are in the same order, thus linking alchemy with the Qabalistic tradition (see Figure 3 and Figure 4).

The controversial Comte de St. Germain (*circa* 1710-1784), allegedly the son of Prince Ragoczy of Transylvania, and a frequent visitor to the courts of Europe, claimed to have knowledge of the Philosopher's Stone and went to great lengths to preserve a sense of mystery so that many thought him immortal. He is nevertheless reputedly the author of a work entitled *The Most Holy Trinosophia* which remains one of the most amazing alchemic tracts known. The following is only an extract and, needless to say, does not adequately convey the magnificence of the work, which covers the entire mystical journey:

> "I crossed the place and mounting on a marble platform which was before me, I noticed with astonishment that I had re-entered the hall of Thrones (the first in which I had found myself when entering the Palace of Wisdom).The triangular altar was still in the centre of this hall but the bird, the altar and the torch were joined and formed a single body. Near them was a golden sun. The sword which I had brought from the hall of fire lay a few paces distant on the cushion of one of the thrones: I took up the sword and struck the sun, reducing it to dust. I then touched it and each molecule became a golden sun like the one I had broken. At that instant a loud and melodious voice exclaimed,' The work is perfect!' Hearing this, the children of light hastened to join me, the doors of immortality were opened to me, and the cloud which covers the eyes of mortals was dissipated. I SAW and the spirits which preside over the elements knew me for their master."

All of the above were aspirants to the Gnosis and perpetuators of a tradition which had a common goal. However, there remains one school of thought which above all others has most influenced the Western Mystery teachings. Like Gnosticism it describes a series of emanations from God which man must retrace – from his lowly position in the material world back to the illuminated Source of All Things. We refer, of course, to the doctrine of the Ancient of Days – the Qabalah.

Figure 3: 'The Universal Way' – painting from *Splendor Solis* by Solomon Trismosin.

Figure 4: 'Transformation of Earth' – painting from *Splendor Solis* by Solomon Trismosin.

III

QABALAH IN THEORY AND PRACTICE

The Qabalah is sometimes said to be the 'yoga' of the Western Tradition inasmuch as it provides for the student both a theoretical framework upon which to hang the most complicated of cosmologies or mythologies, and a practical technique of evolvement.[1] It is based upon the ancient wisdom of Israel, but draws for its content from many Traditions, those of Chaldaea, the Egyptian Mysteries, the Tyrian Mysteries, the wisdom of the Babylonian Magi, the teachings of the Essenes, the Greek and Christian Gnosis, the mathematical theology of Pythagoras, and in later days, the teachings of Rosicrucianism and Alchemy, all blended with the various mythological systems of Europe to make a composite and rich working whole. It is fitting that Israel should have been the basis for the whole metaphysical edifice, as Israel has provided the ground from which Christianity sprung, and is thus indirectly the seed culture of Western civilisation. In addition Israel was the only exoterically Monotheistic religion of the period from which such a system could have sprung. It is *exoterically* Monotheistic, because other religions of the time were Monotheistic in their essence, that is, *esoterically* Monotheistic.

The Qabalah presents in a symbolic form the essential principles not only of Man, but also of God and the Universe. It embraces the gods and goddesses of all other pantheons, which are seen in the Qabalah as aspects of the One God, using them as symbols to express ultimate realities: the forces and forms of the Universe. The Qabalah offers concrete images to express abstract truths in a manner that allows for a latitude of interpretation suited to the individual working with it, and his level of spiritual awareness. The myths that are incorporated in the Qabalah can yield a parable, a science, a philosophy, and a spiritual reality; according to the depth at which they are realised.

The Qabalah is a tradition that has been passed on verbally by learned Jews and rabbis, with its origin lost in antiquity. As the word QBLH in Hebrew literally means 'to receive from mouth to ear', it has been preserved mainly in the form of a verbal tradition, passed on from teacher to pupil under strict vows of secrecy. Even when it has been partly committed to paper it loses little of this secrecy.

The Qabalah is divided into four main sections:

---

[1] But of course there are no parallel physical practices, so this saying can only be construed in the limited sense of a spiritual system of attainment.

(I) The practical Qabalah, which deals with its application in Magic.

(II) The Dogmatic Qabalah, which contains the doctrinal part of the Qabalah, consisting of several main texts with their dependencies. These include the *Zohar*, the *Sepher Yetzirah*, the *Sepher Sephiroth*, and *Aesch Metzareph*.

(III) The Unwritten Qabalah, consisting of the oral knowledge concerning the correct attribution of the symbols to the Tree of Life.

(IV) The Literal Qabalah consists of the three methods of elucidating texts according to the relationship between letters and numbers. In this interpretation, every word and letter of the text is given a numeration, which is then manipulated by the methods of Gematria, Notariqon and Temura to produce 'esoteric' interpretations. Christian examples of this numeration of words are found in the *Book of Revelation*.

The Qabalistic Tradition has survived in the form of manuscript fragments and glyphs, which at first sight appear unintelligible, but upon meditation gradually reveal their inner meanings; thus preserving the teaching in a form that is compact and safe from misuse, but which will deliver its meaning to the aspirant who works hard enough at the glyph. As the racial dharma of the West is control of the physical plane, the system of evolvement chosen by the Westerner should be one that fits this particular destiny, a destiny of accepting life and not escaping it: thus the Western aspirant works with ceremonial Magic – the bringing down of the Godhead to illumine the physical plane, the manifestation of the Divine Law on Earth, not simply an escape from the physical in search of the spiritual.

The first traces of this essentially verbal tradition in a written form appeared *circa* the 3rd century of the Christian Era, in the form of *Sepher Yetzirah* (or *The Book of Creation*). This curious work details the formation of existence in terms of 'Names of Power' with which God sealed the various quarters of the Universe. It has been interpreted variously as a commentary on *Genesis*, a philosophical treatise on the Names of God and the letters of the Hebrew alphabet, or as an instruction whereby man himself could learn to create.

This last interpretation has led to a number of stories concerning that mysterious figure, the Golem. The Golem was a figure created from earth (just as some commentaries of *Genesis* have it that man was), animated with a soul (in the Hebrew sense of Nephesh) which though dumb, could carry out basic chores. By the 12th century the technique for Golem-making had become quite established: one such recipe is to be found in a manuscript in the British Museum by Pseudo-Saadia:[1]

> "They make a circle around the creatures and walk around the circle and recite the 221 alphabets, as they are noted, and some say that the Creator put power into the letters, so that a man makes a creature from virgin earth and kneads it and buries it in the ground, draws a circle and a sphere around the creature, and each time he goes around it recites one of the alphabets. This he should do 462 times. If he walks forward, the creature rises up alive, by virtue of the power inherent in the recitation of the letters. But if he wishes to destroy what he has made, he goes round backwards, reciting the same alphabets from end to beginning. Then the creature sinks into the ground of itself and dies. And so it happened that R. Z.[2] and his students, who busied themselves with the *Book Yetzirah*, by mistake went around backwards, until they themselves by the power of the letters sank into the earth up to their navels. They were unable to escape and cried out. Their teacher heard them and said: 'Recite the letters of the alphabet and walk forward, instead of going backward as you have been doing.' They did so and were released."

A more universally accepted method of endowing the Golem with life was to inscribe the word *emeth*, literally *truth*, on its forehead, so that when its demise is desirable one only has to wipe out the *aleph* which converts the word to *meth* (so that the meaning is altered to 'God alone is truth', implying that the Golem isn't a true creation) and the Golem crumbles back to dust. Of all the rabbis famous for this operation, perhaps Rabbi Loew of Prague has more than his fair share of Golem legends attached to his name.[3]

In modern times Golem-making is usually a matter of using an Elemental, of which more later, to indwell a wax or clay figure which is used in a manner similar to that of a pentacle. In other words the elementary force is

---

[1] British Museum No. 754 in Margoliouth's *Catalogue of Hebrew Manuscripts*.
[2] Rabbi Zadok probably.
[3] See for example *The Miraculous Deeds of Rabbi Loew with the Golem*, Judah Rosenberg, 1909, and *Der Prager Golem*, Chayim Bloch, Berlin, 1920.

'earthed' in the figure so that the magician can continue to reinforce it, using the figure as a storage battery. When the magician has need of the elementary force he unwraps the Golem, as he would unwrap a pentacle, and directs the force into those channels in which it is needed. A number of literary works built around the Golem have been written, of which the most outstanding is Gustav Meyrink's *Der Golem*.

Returning to the development of the Qabalah we find that the next book of any Qabalistic import was published in Southern France around 1180. This book, *Bahir*, Gershom Scholem refers to as 'the earliest Qabalistic document', and is interesting because it includes the first detailed reference to 'tree', 'source', and similar basic Qabalistic symbolism.

However the crown of Qabalistic literature appeared shortly after this, *circa* 1280, as the *Zohar*, or *Book of Splendour*, allegedly written by Moses de Leon. This compilation of 'fourteen camel loads' was of such extent and complexity as to appear to be a collation of a number of previously existing Midrashim (Rabbinical commentaries on the Pentateuch). It is possible however that the bulk[1] of the *Zohar* could have been written by the same author. It is from this enormous storehouse of Qabalistic wisdom that most of the subsequent treatises on the Qabalah have been based.

Some of the most notable Qabalists since then have included Moses Cordovero, Isaac Luria, Abraham Ibn Wakar, Rabbi Hayyim Vital, who wrote some of the most lucid works on the Qabalah of this period,[2] and Solomon Ibn Gebirol, the famed author of *Me'qor Hayyim*. The last-named book is better known as *Fons Vitae*, or the *Fountain of Life*,[3] a book that has also strongly influenced Christian thinking.

Outside of this strictly Rabbinical tradition, other writers, including quite a few Christians, wrote treatises on the Qabalah. These included John Baptist von Helmont, of early scientific fame; Raymond Lully, author of *Ars Magna*; Baruch Spinoza, the 'God-intoxicated philosopher'; Pico di Mirandola; Knorr von Rosenroth, the author of *Kabbala Denudata*, and in

---

[1] The main parts of the *Zohar* including *Midrash ha-Neelam*, the *Idra Rabba*, *Idra Zutta*, *Sitre Torah*, and most of the shorter treatises.

[2] Rabbi Hayyim Vital wrote *The Gate of Heaven*, *The Book of Enoch*, *Pardes Rimmonium*, *A Treatise on the Emanations*, and *Otz ha Chiim*.

[3] For a translation and commentary on this work, see Isaac Meyer, *Qabbalah, the Philosophical Writings of Avicebron*, Stuart, London, 1970. Other books from this period include those by Isaac Luria, *Rashith ha Gilgalim*; Rabbi Akiba, *The Alphabet*; and Rabbi Azariel ben Menachem, *The Commentary on the Ten Sephiroth*.

England, Henry More, the Cambridge Platonist.[1]

Amongst this rapidly proliferating tradition there grew up the Rosicrucian tradition, allegedly brought from Damcar by one Christian Rosencreutz. This almost mythical figure was introduced to the public by two documents, *Fama Fraternitatis* (published in 1614) and *Confessione Fraternitatis R.C.* (published a year later), which traced the wanderings of Fra. C.R.C., as Christian Rosencreutz was called. He travelled from Germany, through Jerusalem and Damascus, to Damcar, where he learned Mathematics, Medicine (Physic) and Philosophy, as well as transcribing that often-mentioned, but rarely seen, *Book M.* He left Damcar for Fez where he learned from the 'Arabians' both the Qabalah and Magic, which were here closely associated with each other.

Upon returning to Germany via Spain, Christian Rosencreutz established an Order for the preservation and propagation of the Wisdom he had learned in the East. This Order kept its existence secret for over 100 years, till the two manifestoes mentioned above were published.

Since then however there has been no lack of societies, orders and brotherhoods claiming the exalted title of Rosicrucian, down to the present day when there are at least four organisations who claim this style, and who will admit you, for a fee, to the Rosicrucian Mysteries, by post; not to mention many others which are less well publicised.

The original order survived in Germany under several Masonic and Rosicrucian designations, sending forth at least one branch to another country. This branch, despite the many and varied stories of its foundations, came into existence in England in the last two decades of the 19th century.

This Order was the Hermetic Order of the Golden Dawn, whose early inception has been too often reiterated to bear repetition in this book. Suffice it to say that it drew its extensive heritage of esoteric information from several English Freemasons, including Frederick Hockley, Robert Wentworth Little and Kenneth Mackenzie, who had earlier, in 1865, formed the Societas Rosicruciana in Anglia. This knowledge was supplemented by that of S.L. Macgregor Mathers, an erudite Qabalist, who

---

[1] Other Qabalists of this period include Pope Sixtus IV, Johannes Reuchlin (*De Verbo Mirifico* and *De Arte Cabalistica*), Robert Fludd, the Jesuit Athanasius Kircher, John Pistorius, Henry Cornelius Agrippa, Jerome Cardan, Gulielmus Postellus, and Thomas Vaughan.

together with Dr. Woodman and Wynn Westcott were issued a charter to form an English temple for 'instruction in the mediaeval Occult Sciences' by Anna Sprengel and Dr. Thiesen of Leige, members of a German Rosicrucian Order.[1] (See Figure 8.)

Accordingly in 1887 the first Isis-Urania Temple of the Hermetic Students of the Golden Dawn was formed. Of the original three chiefs, we hear little of Dr. Woodman, but both Macgregor Mathers and Wynn Westcott put much effort into expanding the work of the Order in the light of their own learning.[2]

Subsequent developments included the death of Dr. Woodman (1891) and the resignation of Wynn Westcott (1897), leaving the Order with Mathers as head, and with branch Temples at Bradford, Edinburgh, Weston-super-Mare, and Paris (all except the last two being short-lived).

From this Order sprang most of the work done on Magic, the Qabalah, and the Western Esoteric Tradition in the 20th century. It is therefore important that we examine the techniques of this Order, as they have had such an influence over the search for Abraxas in the West.

The practices of the Golden Dawn, as they were based on the Qabalah and German Rosicrucianism, had as their central glyph 'the Tree of Life'. The Tree of Life, or Otz Chiim, is a diagrammatic system of the relationships that exist between everything in Man and the Universe: it is applicable to both because the principles upon which both manifested are the same.

This glyph portrays creation as the Great Unmanifest manifesting in a series of emanations, outflowing from the three Veils of Negative Existence. These emanations follow the order of the Lightning Flash and in doing so 'God incarnates in the Universe', and the infinite becomes finite through limitation.

Each of these emanations, or Sephiroth, can variously be interpreted as an aspect of the Godhead, a stage in creation, or a facet in the constitution of man.

This multiple identification arises from the doctrine (as expressed by Hermes Trismegistus): "As above, so below, but after another fashion."[3]

---

[1] W. Wynn Westcott, *Data of the History of the Rosicrucians*, London, 1916.
[2] S.L. Macgregor Mathers, *The Kabbalah Unveiled*, and Wynn Wescott, *An Introduction to the Study of the Kabbalah*, have become classics of the subject.
[3] Hermes Trismegistus, *Smaragdine Tablet*.

By this it is meant that the Universe contains different forms of existence, each using the same blueprint, and it is held that because of this similar blueprinting, an examination of any part of the Universe at a particular time should reveal, by analogy, the forces pertaining to the whole, and so to other parts of the Universe. In the Hermetic sense, the structure of the microcosm (the inner world) is similar in outline to the structure of the macrocosm (the outer world).

A close modern analogy to this would be to point out, as James Jeans has, that the structure of the atom, that of the solar system, and that of a nebula, are in principle the same. This vision of 'wheels within wheels' characterise much of the form of some chemically induced visions,[1] which will be mentioned in a later chapter.

Returning to the Tree of Life, and applying this Hermetic axiom to it, it becomes apparent why the infinite abundance of images and symbols attributed to it explain every facet of reality and unreality in the Universe, no matter how large or how small. It also becomes apparent why the motto taken by Macgregor Mathers, "There is no part of me which is not of the Gods," was an expression of his philosophy rather than an idle boast.

It is therefore very difficult to attempt to compress a description of this glyph in so short a compass, and the reader would be well advised to fill in the following sketch of the system by consulting such books as Dion Fortune's *Mystical Qabalah* or Macgregor Mathers' *Kabbalah Unveiled.*

The glyph Otz Chiim (see Figure 5) is divided into 10 Spheres and 22 Paths (lines connecting them), attributed to the 22 Letters of the Hebrew Alphabet, or the 12 Signs of the Zodiac, together with the seven Planets of the Ancients, and the three Elements (of the four Classical Elements, Fire, Air, Water, Earth). The fourth Element, Earth, does not appear on the Paths but is attributed to the physical plane and is therefore not among the Paths that lead into the Unseen.

The 22 Atus, or Major Arcana of the Tarot, are also ascribed to the 22 Paths of the Tree. The significance of these Paths can be deduced by the two Spheres that a given Path relates or connects, and the Tarot Trump ascribed to it.

The ten Spheres or Sephiroth generate from the Three Veils of Negative

---

[1] Specifically ether-induced visions.

Existence to form the Primal Point or First Manifestation, Kether the Crown of Creation. Kether, asexual in nature, divides into Binah and Chokmah, and with this division forms a functional trinity that can then proceed to generate. This pair Chokmah and Binah respectively equate to the archetypal Male and Female potencies. At this stage a balance is achieved, the triad being considered in the Qabalah as a balanced number: collectively these three are called the three Supernals.

The product of Chokmah and Binah is a phenomenal existence that Kether could never achieve by itself. From these sprang a Sephirah which is given no number: Daath, the Sephirah which hangs above the Abyss, separating the three Supernals (which partake of the nature of God) from the rest of the Tree (which partakes of the nature of Man). Daath is in another dimension, so it has not got the same kind of 'existence' that the other Sephiroth have: it was the first child of Binah and Chokmah, and preceded the emanation of the seven Lower Sephiroth.

It is necessary to have *three* Sephiroth before generation of the phenomenal Universe can commence, just as it is necessary to have three straight lines to enclose a space. The third Sephirah, Binah, therefore makes the phenomenal Universe possible by introducing Time as a limiting factor: hence Chronos or Saturn is ascribed to it.

The three Supernals are the Head of Adam Kadmon (the Archetypal Man) and are separate from the rest of the Sephiroth, but yet form the principle upon which all else manifests – the Principle of the Trinity. The Trinity occurs again in the Ethical Triad of Chesed, Geburah and Tiphareth and in the Astral Triad of Netzach, Hod and Yesod.

Chokmah heads the Pillar of Mercy (Male) and Binah the Pillar of Severity (Female), whilst Kether heads the Pillar of Equilibrium (Androgyne or Hermaphrodite). Thus the Principle of the balance of opposites by a reconciling factor is established in the Tree. This balance is the balance between Force (Chokmah) and Form (Binah), just as science sees the Universe as a balance between energy and matter. As the vertex of the Supernal Triangle points towards the Ain Soph Aur, its balance derives from that which lies beyond the Veils, whilst the two other Triangles of the Tree have down-pointing vertices, showing their dependence upon the manifested phenomenal Universe for their *raison d'être*: this shows even more distinctly the function of the Abyss.

After the failure of Daath, Chesed (Mercy) was generated. Out of this Sephirah sprang its opposite, Geburah (Severity), and the two of these unified in the down-pointing triangle, whose apex is Tiphareth (Beauty).

To each of these in turn is ascribed Jupiter with its qualities of construction, expansion and solidification, the merciful ruler (Chesed); Mars, the transition by destruction of forms or ideas into materials for the construction of further forms (Geburah); and the Sun, the centre of both the Tree and our solar system, the beauty and harmony of the sacrifice of its energies for Life (Tiphareth).

A division on the Tree similar, on a lower arc, to the Abyss, is the Veil Paroketh which separates Hod and Netzach from Tiphareth, symbolising on the microcosmic level the point to which man may attain whilst yet remaining human. Macrocosmically the Veil separates the Sephiroth Hod and Netzach, its opposite, from their reconciliation in Tiphareth. Tiphareth, incidentally, is also the Redeemer not only of the Ethical Triangle, but also of the whole Tree: it is the Son, just as Kether is the Father, and Yesod the Holy Spirit. It is situated at the heart of the Tree.

So far we have formed a Hexagram with the upward apex of Kether (the Father) reflected in the downward-pointing apex of Tiphareth (the Son). Tiphareth now forms the head of a Calvary cross, whose foot rests on the Earth at Malkuth and whose opposite arms are Netzach (Victory) and Hod (Glory).

Netzach, to which Venus is attributed, represents the elemental sphere of Nature's forces, or in the constitution of man, the unconscious. Opposing it on the other Pillar of the Tree is Hod, attributed to Mercury and covering the mercurial processes of thinking and rationality. Slung between these two, on the Middle Pillar and completing the Triad, is the ninth Sephirah, Yesod (Foundation).

Yesod, whose symbol is the Moon, is the reconciler of Netzach (Nature Mysticism) and Hod (Intellectual Magic) in its capacity as the Sephirah of psychism. Yesod's place in the Universe is that of the 'darkly splendid treasure house of images', in Theosophical imagery, the Astral Plane. This is both the Foundation of the Tree and the repository of the illusions of the Universe.

This concept reflects the Eastern view that 'all is Maya', in that the Universe is here seen as *based* on illusion. The Qabalistic rationale of this is that the Universe has been generated from the archetypal images generated in the mind of the Logos (literally the 'Word' in *St. John*, Chap. 1, v. 1), which is seen by the Qabalist not only as God, but as God's means of creating the Universe through the vibration of a sound.[1] The Qabalistic doctrine of the Word plays an important part in the practical Qabalah, that is, in Magic. As in all invocations and evocations the accurate 'vibration' of 'Words of Power' is the crux and quite often the climax of a ritual designed to produce a particular change in consciousness.[2]

Consequently it is not surprising that the magical philosophy claims that basic changes in consciousness, if not in matter itself, can be wrought by a change in vibrations. The vibration of 'Words of Power' is no mere chanting or shouting aloud, but the warmth and the trembling that can be felt in the body and the shaking of the temple in which they are pronounced.

But to return from this digression, the last Sephirah of the Tree of Life is pendant to Yesod, in the sense that, if it were not there, the Tree would be perfectly symmetrical. It, however, provides for the descent of the powers, images, and planes of existence, summarised by the Tree, into the material world. The Sephiroth are not to be interpreted as different spatial areas, but as levels of consciousness or awareness interpenetrating each other, but distinct in that the 'laws' of each sphere are completely different.[3] The Tree has, in addition to the relationships between the Paths and Spheres, a fourfold nature.

---

[1] Vide *Genesis*, Chap. I, v. 3: "and God said, Let there be light: and there was light."

[2] A possibly irrelevant but interesting observation is that science is increasingly explaining the ultimate particles of matter in terms of vibration, rather than existence as a finite lump of matter. In fact as Einstein proved in 1905, matter is entirely inter-convertible with energy, and energy is very much a matter of waves or vibrations.

[3] Howard Hinton's book, *The Fourth Dimension*, and Dunne's *An Experiment with Time*, exemplify a scientific approach to dimensions of time and space seen as distinct but interpenetrating.

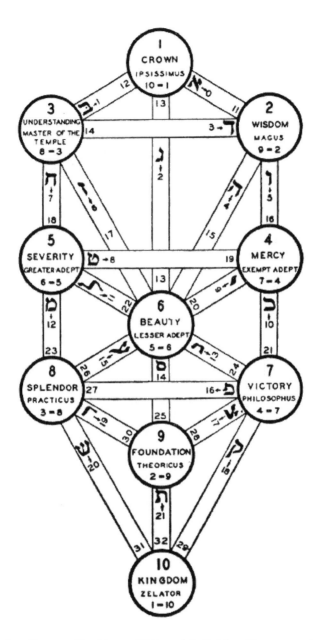

Figure 5: Otz Chiim – The Tree of Life, with Golden Dawn magical grades, and Hebrew letters on the 22 Paths.

This is produced by considering the Tree under four different aspects, or as the Qabalists say, in Four Worlds. The Spheres each exist in each of these Worlds which are called, from the most ethereal to the most material:

(1) *Atziluth*, the Archetypal World or World of Emanations: in which the Sephiroth have a Godname ascribed to them.

(2) *Briah*, the World of Creation, or *Khorsia*, the World of Thrones: in which each Sphere has ascribed to it one of the Ten Archangels. In this World the Archetypal Ideations of the Godhead in Atziluth are brought unformed into creation.

(3) *Yetzirah*, the World of Formation and of Angels: in which each Sphere has ascribed to it an Angelic Host. In this World the formlessness of the Briatic World is ordered and diversified into elements, as symbolised by the Angelic Host.

(4) *Assiah*, the World of Action, the World of Matter (not exclusively physical): in which each Sphere has ascribed to it a Mundane Chakra. The Mundane Chakras (not to be confused with the Yogic term) are, in order from Kether to Malkuth, the 'Primum Mobile', the Zodiac, the seven planets of the Ancients (Binah to Yesod), with Malkuth as the Four Elements taken together. Each Sphere has a mode of existence in each of the Four Worlds, thus making 40 Sephiroth in all.

The Paths and Spheres are given their order by two symbols that sometimes appear on the Tree, they are:

(1) The fiery sword or Lightning Flash, which gives the order of Sephiroth, or Macrocosmic aspects of the Tree. This shows the Cosmic Path of Involution.

(2) The Serpent Nehushtan, which gives the correct order of the Paths, or the Microcosmic aspects of the Tree. This shows the Path of Evolution that has to be pursued by the consciousness of Man, or specifically the order of initiation pursued by the Western aspirant.

In addition to the Paths and Sephiroth, there are two elements that are beyond the 'dimension of the Tree'; these are the Abyss (alternatively, the hidden Sephirah Daath) and the three Veils of Negative Existence. These Veils are a 'backdrop' against which the structure of the Tree is built: they both symbolise and remove the necessity of postulating an Absolute. This paradox is explained when it is realised that in one sense they constitute the turning point between Negative and Positive Existence, just as the digit zero is required to bridge the gap between the positive and negative numerals, yet in itself it means nothing – it is merely a convenient cipher to represent the unimaginable no-thing. Also the three Veils remove the necessity of going further back, as they provide a convenient point of reference that is fixed and not shifting (like the indefinite 'Absolute' of most philosophies).

The limiting of the Tree by the Veils makes the Tree take a finite form, so that its symbols can be used in the Qabalistic method as a chain of associated ideas that can lead the student to a realisation of abstract concepts, arising from a visual symbol system.

Negative Manifestation transmutes through Negativity (Ain), Limitlessness (Ain Soph) and Limitless Light (Ain Soph Aur) to one effulgent point of brilliance which is the first positive manifestation, Kether, the Crown of manifestation. The nine Sephiroth that follow are phases of involution. This contrasts with the subjective nature of the interconnecting Paths which are the evolving soul's apprehension of the Cosmos, as well as the Path of return that it must take to reach Abraxas.

The Emanations, or Sephiroth, evolve each from the previous one, so that all the Sephiroth are held in potential in the Ain Soph Aur, each Sephiroth being emanated when the previous one has formed sufficiently to react to the unbalanced nature of its birth by overflowing to form the next lowest Sephirah.

God, in a sense, is the compulsion to expand outwards[1] into manifestation, and it is the uprushing from the Great Unmanifest, rather than the separate and complete fashioning of each article (as portrayed in *Genesis*) that constitutes the essence of Creation. Overflow into the new expression of the Life-force (the new Sephirah) occurs when the manifesting energy has run through all possible expressions of itself at the level of the previous Sephirah, from which the new one springs. Thus, for example, the nodal expression of the Life-force in Kether (Rashith ha Gilgalim or First Swirlings) takes a new expression when it forms Chokmah, in which the circular movement has the concept of segmentation (Mazloth, the Zodiac) added to it to form this new Sephirah.

---

[1] The Sanskrit *Brāhm* means 'to expand', hence *Brahma*.

Just as the Sephiroth represent the generation or involution of the Godhead into material existence, so the Paths indicate the path of evolution or return to the Godhead, the path along which many in the West seek Abraxas. The training of an aspirant in the Western Tradition is designed to give him a full knowledge of his own psyche: and having attained this, to strengthen each facet in turn. It has been said by the Yoga philosophy that the most spiritual and powerful aspect of man's nature is the faculty of attention or consciousness. As the most fundamental aspect of man's free will is the choice of what he allows his attention to dwell upon, it is the goal of Yogic practice to "discover and directly experience the nature of the attention or faculty of consciousness by which all else is known." Likewise in the West the first training involves meditation and concentration.

This may take the form of simple visualisations held for only short periods of time. It is often surprising for the beginner how really undisciplined his mind is: even to picture a red triangle for more than a few minutes without losing sight of a side or two, or being distracted by other thoughts, is difficult.

However, it is essential that the ability to concentrate on ordinary things is brought to perfection as it is a major weapon in the Adept's armoury. The reason for this is that the next level of subtleness above the physical plane (ignoring the etheric level), the Astral plane, is the level of images, an objective Universe of plastic thought, corresponding to Yesod.

Although this is a facile interpretation, basically the Astral plane is the first level of non-normal consciousness that the aspirant learns to work with, or put subjectively, the first portion of his subconscious that he contacts. One of the laws of this plane is that concentrated thought on a particular form will endure in the astral in proportion to the amount of concentration exerted. Armed with this ability to concentrate, the aspirant now needs to be able to select that part of the astral which he proposes to investigate. Bear in mind at this point that his 'explorations' of the astral are, in fact, explorations of himself, in accordance with the dictum *gnōthi seauton* or 'know thyself' which hung over the portals of the Eleusinian Mysteries.

Of the several methods for directing the attention of the consciousness to various parts of the astral, the best known are 'skrying' or 'spirit vision' and ceremonial magic. The first consists of taking a symbol attributed to that aspect of consciousness which is to be investigated and visualising it strongly, as if it were a door set into an interminably long wall. It is here that one's ability to visualise and hold a picture becomes paramount, for the symbol may be anything from a simple coloured triangle as in the Tattwa cards to a complex esoteric Tarot card.

Commencing with the simplest, Tattwa cards are symbolic expressions of the Four Elements[1] of the ancients, already mentioned, together with the Fifth Element of Akasha or 'Spirit'. These symbols have been adopted into the Western system from the East as gates to the astral manifestations of these Forces which have the *qualities* of the physical elements to which they are referred. The Akasha is considered the progenitor of the other four elements, of which the 'first-born' is *Tejas* or Fire, whose symbol is an upward-pointing red triangle and which signifies the energy, expansion and consuming properties of fire. This Element of Fire manifests throughout the Universe and is not constrained to the element of fire.

The second Tattwa is *Vayu*, the principle of Air, which is a balance between the opposing Elements of Fire and Water,[2] and therefore expresses the qualities of the overlying mantle in which the Earth is drowned. The symbol of Air is a blue circle.

Similarly, Water, *Apas*, is symbolised by a silver Moon crescent and Earth, *Prithevi*, by a solid yellow square.

Now these symbols can be taken in combination so that *Tejas* of *Apas* would be the red triangle of *Tejas*, superimposed on the silver crescent of *Apas*, making a total of 25 possible combinations of Tattwas. In using these as portals to the subconscious one paints the symbol on a card with a background of the complementary colour. After staring at it for some time, transfer the vision to a white background on which is seen the negative after-image. The negative after-image should then be seized upon by the imagination and portrayed as a translucent doorway. After giving the sign of the grade appropriate to the element and using a short invocation of an appropriate nature, one waits patiently for the door to swing open.

When it does, the skryer will be met with a landscape whose nature is in accordance with the nature of the Tattwa. If, for example, the skryer was skrying with *Tejas* of *Prithevi*, or Fire of Earth, a vision of a sandy desert stretching into the distance and lit by the lurid glare of fires roaring on the

---

[1] The Elements are *Tejas* – Fire; *Vayu* – Air; *Apas* – Water; *Prithevi* – Earth.
[2] See *Sepher Yetzirah*.

horizon, reflected by heavy dull clouds hanging low in the air, might greet him. Upon stepping, mentally, through the portal he would find the rough ground beneath his feet warm and firm, the air oppressive with heat, and perhaps the feeling that he was not entirely alone. A figure not unlike a combination of the Gnome and Salamander of medieval tales might appear and guide him through the landscape which is symbolic of the work of that sub-Element; in this case the volcanic action required to produce metal ores in rocks is one such aspect. When the skryer has seen enough he should retread the same path back to the astral 'doorway', the Tattwa image through which he came. Then being very careful to return slowly and definitely to the physical plane, he passes through the doorway, visualises it closing behind him and completes the operation with a Banishing Ritual.

It is interesting to note that the personification of the forces of the elements in the Middle Ages closely resembles the forms which greet a skryer who ventures into these realms: It is conceivable that many tales of fairies, gnomes, sylphs and so on can be explained in terms of the author having had a natural psychic ability so that what may have seemed a dream to him was actually an experience of a realm of Elemental force, which provides the raw energy of Nature but which is seldom encountered on its own terms. The skryer, with practice, finds he is able to explore at greater length the realm of the elements and become acquainted with the Elementals therein. It was to these *personifications* of the forces of Nature that we referred when discussing the Golem.

Elementals, being of a substance closer to the physical than most other types of existence included in the Tree of Life, are obviously more amenable to 'earthing' or manifesting on the material plane. However, other portals to the astral may be used, the image or figure used in each case being a type of *psycho-active* glyph, a figure which has significance to our subconscious mind or, even deeper, to our archetypal unconsciousness. These glyphs, drawn from Qabalistic symbols, range from Hebrew letters (portals to the Paths of the Tree), the Tarot (of which those cards easily available are simplified compared with some packs used for the purposes of skrying), the dots of Geometric figures, the figures of the *I Ching*, Tattwa symbols, some alchemical illustrations,[1] and drawings by some artists who have a knowledge of the workings of the psyche at its

---

[1] Especially those from Solomon Trismosin's *Splendor Solis*. See Figure 3 and Figure 4..

deeper levels.

It is interesting to note that the Tarot, Geomancy, and the *I Ching* are all modes of divination and the first two were used for this purpose by the Order. Geomancy consists of figures made up of four different groups of odd and even points, making a total of 16 different figures which are derived by a random method of selection.

The Tarot, however, is an infinitely more complex instrument, as it contains 78 symbols, capable of being combined in approximately 10^{21} different ways, yielding a much more flexible system of divination. The Tarot has been too well documented elsewhere to elaborate on it here, except to point out that the books listed in the bibliography by Paul Case, Gareth Knight and Aleister Crowley are good introductions to the subject.

Moving now from subjective working with divination and skrying, we come to one of the main facets of the Practical Qabalah, ceremonial magic. This entails the exaltation of the consciousness by using a barrage of sense impressions, of a similar type, designed to focus the mind on to a particular phase of mentation to the exclusion of all others. At this point the ritual either fails, or unites the consciousness of the practitioner (microcosm) to the corresponding potency in the Universe (macrocosm) and there is a flow through of energy which *illuminates* that particular facet of the practitioner's consciousness.

These stimuli are the bare bones of magical ritual, along with the conditioning of the mind to the symbols of the Mysteries, for if the ritual has been designed correctly then these stimuli and symbols should be of a similar symbolic nature. Thus if the magical operation was designed to cause a change of consciousness in one of the participants, to loosen up his perhaps overly intellectual approach to life, and free subconscious blocks which were inhibiting his emotional responses, then an operation of the sphere of Netzach might be undertaken.

Accordingly, the physical stimuli of the ritual would consist of circle and triangle inscribed with those words which are appropriate to the evocation of a 'spirit' corresponding to the seventh Sephirah, Netzach. The instruments used would be the Lamp and the Girdle, the perfumes used would be either benzoin, rose or red sandal, all luxurious odours. The spirit evoked would correspond to that portion of the practitioner's psyche which it was desired to 'free'. Invocation, on the other hand, would, in the case of this sphere, be addressed to these ancient personifications of Universal forces which would be represented, in the case of Netzach, by Venus, in the Roman Pantheon, Aphrodite in the Greek, and Hathor in the Egyptian Pantheon.

If the ritualised representations of these forces succeed, then the Vision of beauty triumphant, the flush of elation as the impeded emotions break free, and the race of the pulse as the consciousness exalts in its new freedom, greet the practitioner.

Thus the Qabalist uses concrete symbols to call up in the mind associated ideas and feelings which gradually form connected chains of thought which lead the mind into the abstract realms of thought without demanding of the student that he grasp the abstract with nothing more to aid him than his concrete mind. Thus the abstract concept is ensnared within the concrete network of symbols. The identification of the mind with these abstracts establishes a link between the aspirant and the reservoir of force associated with the abstractions.

Just as the electrician needs a detailed knowledge of the properties of electricity (although as yet no scientist can explain what electricity really is) before he is able to design circuits necessary to carry out certain functions, so the magician uses the Qabalistic knowledge concerning other forces in the Universe, in his techniques.

This then is ceremonial magic. It differs from the Eastern forms of illumination in that the ceremonial on the physical plane acts as a psychological stimulant to focus and intensify a particular type of force. The symbols derived from the Tree of Life are used to select and concentrate the different types of force symbolised by the Paths and Spheres of the Tree. When the aspirant achieves *mastery* of a particular Sphere of the Tree he has access to all the differing manifestations of this type of force in other Traditions that go to make up the complex Western Tradition. Hence the aspirant gains knowledge successively of each part of his psyche and the corresponding universal potency. This contrasts with Eastern practice which attempts to eliminate all concepts, symbols and modes of rational mentation in an endeavour to reach Ultimate Reality by subtraction of symbols.

Each system is valid, one seeking to expand cognition by experiencing all levels of consciousness, the other by the exclusion of the many sensory and mental distractions which prevent the attention focusing on that conceptless state which is the source of the phenomenal Universe. To reach back to the origin, so say the Qabalists, one must either expand to include all, or contract to a focus.

One such seeker for Abraxas was Aleister Crowley who joined the Golden Dawn on 18 November 1898. At his initiation he took the Magical Name of Perdurabo, literally, 'I will endure': and endure he did, to the end of his 72 years, the scorn and hatred of the world, the epithet of the 'Wickedest Man in the World', and a continued misinterpretation of his philosophy and work. Even his simplest statements were misconstrued by a public eager to find a Black Magician or a Satanist in anyone who dared to be so different.

Aleister Crowley's great annunciation, stemming from the *Book of the Law* – "Do What Thou Wilt Shall Be the Whole of the Law" – if interpreted by normally acceptable standards is completely unacceptable, but Crowley meant it in another sense. Crowley defines one's True Will as being the course, dependent partly on self and partly on the environment, which is natural and necessary for each person. He likens each individual to the star which has its own course through the Universe, its own proper motion and character, which very rarely results in a collision with any other star, and pursues its way un-interfered with, except insofar as its course is gravitationally modified by the presence of other stars. Since in the vastnesses of space there are seldom conflicts between celestial bodies, so in the realms of mankind there should be no chaos, little conflict and no mutual disturbance, were each individual aware of his True Will, his purpose in life, and eager to fulfil it. Unfortunately, most men, through lack of an understanding of reality, do not know their True Will and spend their time pursuing chimeras of pleasure, often at their own expense and that of others.

Crowley's corollary to his main dictum, "Love is the Law, Love under Will", annunciates Christ's two commandments, together with the rider that such love should be governed by the requirements of one's force and True Will.

Like all geniuses, there was an unbalanced side to his nature; but why should we expect a balance in a man of spiritual genius as one does not expect it in the fields of art, music or literature? After all, this unbalance manifested only through 'Crowley the man', not in his research and teachings, or through 'Crowley the Mage'. One of Crowley's most noticeable attributes was that he never attempted to hide his most 'socially unacceptable' characteristics. This shows both his supreme disregard for society, and contrasts strongly with other spiritual teachers of the time, who concerned themselves as much with their image as with their illumination.

After travelling in the East, Ceylon, India, and across Southern China, absorbing the techniques of Eastern esotericism, Crowley returned to England to form his own Order, the Argentium Astrum, or A.'. A.'.. Crowley incorporated a number of Yoga practices with those of Western Magic into the structure of the A.'. A.'., forming a single system of attainment.

Of his system Crowley says that the experience of enlightenment, whether obtained by meditation or Magic, is marked by the emergence of an entirely new type of consciousness not differentiated into a subject-object state, for these have been fused into an undivided One. Whatever is seen, heard or felt in these moments is flooded with an inrush from the depths of the inner man. Deep lying powers which are not ordinarily put into play seem suddenly liberated and the usual insulations which sunder and restrict our inner life into separate compartments seem shot through. It is the emergence of a new type-level of life, corresponding in some way with ultimate sources of Reality; it is a surge of the entire Self towards ineffable fullness of life.

From the psychological point of view, the following are true of the experience:

> (1) The results are entirely illogical, from our ordinary point of view, but they give a unique form of knowledge which nothing else will give.

> (2) The mystical states of all men, of different ages, exhibit an extraordinary similarity.

> (3) The experience is related to something which represents Reality.

(4) It produces clear-cut results: *genius*.[1]

The experience produces art and genius in every field of endeavour, because therein all forms seem to speak, and there is gained an immediate intuition of form. One becomes a close and willing observer of Life itself rather than of the externals used by life: from the Beatific Vision one reads the meaning of existence, and by these pictures one trains oneself for life and its appreciation.

The A.'.A.'. did not have many members in its early years, but the monumental body of work left behind by Crowley has provided the Western Tradition with one of ifs most scientifically ordered systems. Since Crowley's death in 1947, the number of people working with his system has greatly increased, especially with the formation of dependent Orders based on Crowley's work, such as the 'Luculentus Astrum', and various recensions of the A.'. A.'..

As we have seen, the doors to the various levels of the consciousness are initially opened, and later recognised, by the sigils, symbols and signs which are archetypally related to them.

Some artists in the 20th century deliberately set out to use this knowledge of the subconscious to draw or paint pictures which can act as keys and unlock particular parts of the psyche, from the shallowest levels to the deepest atavistic memories. One such man was Austin Osman Spare …

---

[1] "Why, with a pen or brush, one man sits down and makes a masterpiece, and yet another, with the selfsame instruments and opportunities, turns out a daub or botch, is twenty times more curious than all the musings of the mystics, works of the Rosicrucians …" Preface by R.B. Cunninghame Graham to *The Canon*, by J. Stirling. Aleister Crowley described this book as "the best text-book of Applied Qabalah."

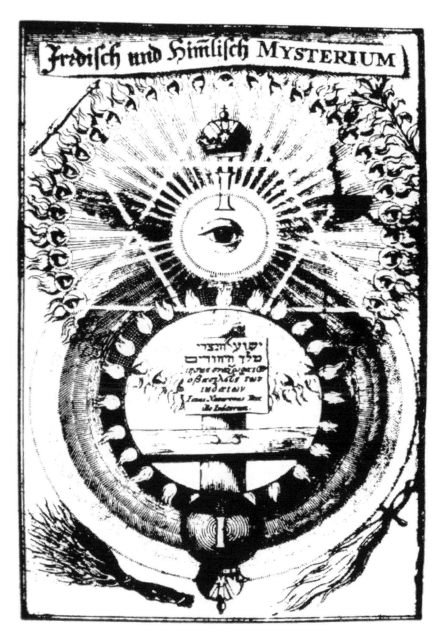

Figure 6: 'The Earthly and Heavenly Mystery' – drawing from *The Works of Jacob Boehme*. The central inscriptions are the words purportedly nailed to Christ's cross.

Figure 7: 'The Tree of the Knowledge of Good and Evil' – drawing from *The Secret Symbols of the Rosicrucians.*

Figure 8: The Rose Cross, central symbol of the Rosicrucian Order of the Golden Dawn.

Figure 9: The Vault of Christian Rosencreutz. *From top left, clockwise:* The Ceiling of the Vault; The Floor of the Vault; The Circular Altar; The Rose and Cross.

Section II
The World of Shadows

"If the depths of our minds conceal strange forces
capable of augumenting or conquering those on the surface,
it is in our greatest interest to capture them."

— André Breton

I

THE STRANGE WORLD OF AUSTIN OSMAN SPARE

Austin Spare, illustrator extraordinary, man of sigils, explorer of atavisms and vehicle for phantoms, was born at midnight on 31 December 1886, in a suburb of London. Today he is beginning to emerge from his posthumous obscurity. His drawings and paintings, demoniac but strangely beautiful, are being rediscovered in the same way that Beardsley's were. His writings, which expound a system of probing the subconscious and the powers latent in man, have not yet been fully explained.[1] The aim of this chapter, therefore, is to present and, it is hoped, provide a useful commentary upon the theories of this remarkable man who died virtually unnoticed in 1956.

Spare was probably the first modern occultist to evolve a self-contained working hypothesis about the nature of psychic energy and its manifestation, which could be applied without all the paraphernalia of traditional rituals, grimoires and magical incantations. His system of sigils shows how an effort of will, when focused on the subconscious, can unleash the most amazing psychic energy. Spare's writing style is complicated and occasionally, like Crowley's, too personalised to fathom. There emerges, however, a certain rationale, which in itself is lucid and simple in conception, and undoubtedly significant in its application: but to return again to the beginning ...

When he was 16, Spare won a scholarship to the Royal College of Art, and in the early years of the 20th century he was commissioned to illustrate a handful of books including Ethel Wheeler's *Behind the Veil* (1906) and a book of aphorisms entitled *The Starlit Mire* (1911). In the early '20s he was co-editor, with Clifford Bax, of an excellent illustrated literary magazine called *The Golden Hind* which ran for eight quarterly issues (1922-24) before being discontinued. It contained a number of Spare's drawings, mostly of sumptuous fleshly women, occasionally shown with atavistic characteristics – some had deer's heads, for example. Also featured were articles by Aldous Huxley, Alec Waugh and Havelock Ellis, as well as illustrations by such brilliant 'decadents' as Harry Clarke, Alastair and John Austen.[2] Despite these encouraging early signs, Spare's life was lived mainly out of the mainstream of contemporary ideas. And it is Spare's

---

[1] Kenneth Grant's *Images and Oracles of Austin Osman Spare* was published by Muller, London, in 1975, three years after the first publication of *The Search for Abraxas*.
[2] There were also other magazines: *Form* edited by Spare and Marsden (1916-17), and *Form* edited by Spare and Davies (1921).

concepts, his own occult philosophy which he wrote down and illustrated admirably in a few now very rare books, that would seem to be the most potent reminder of his genius. His life resembled a vortex caught up within a framework from which it had to burst free to take its fullest effect. Spare's art and philosophy evolves from a traditionalist approach into something quite his own. He moves from a style resembling Edmund J. Sullivan, the well known black and white illustrator, to a frenzy of detail in which both symbols and subject are interfused; from a seemingly orthodox mysticism to an atavistic occultism which involved regressing through countless bestial intrangencies within the subconscious, to the final source of creation.

Spare visited Egypt during World War I and was no doubt strongly impressed by the solemn, magnetic presence of the ancient Egyptian pantheon. Near-Eastern deities of all grades and significance abound in his drawings. But Spare's first book betrays a background most strongly influenced by another, related, mystery tradition: the Qabalah. This brand of Jewish mysticism which modern occultists claim was passed down as a secret tradition concurrent with, if not earlier than, Christianity, has provided the main basis of Western Magic, especially in its outline of various divine names, or 'words of power'. These are verbal representations of an aspect of a deity otherwise too abstract to represent. The order of the Golden Dawn had predominantly Qabalistic leanings and made use of these God names in its rituals, although Egyptian deities were also frequently alluded to. Most significantly for our argument, it is believed that around 1910 Austin Spare was a member of the A.'. A.'. (Argentium Astrum: The Silver Star), an occult group, some of whose teachings Aleister Crowley derived from the Golden Dawn. As far back as the publication in February 1905 of a limited edition of *Earth: Inferno*, Spare had been developing his ideas along at least semi-traditional Qabalistic patterns (although no one would suggest that the Golden Dawn and its derivatives were purely academic).

At this stage Spare tends to be dualistic: he sees things generally as either positive or negative, spiritual or materialistic, real or delusory. Human existence for him is a continuing sequence of lives during which man learns to cope with the problems and adverse situations which arise in direct relation to the ability inherent in his personality. The unenlightened meanwhile become bogged down in empty traditions and activities devoid of vitality. Furthermore they fail to perceive the principle KIA,

Spare's name for 'Ain Soph', which is the one Source behind all manifestation, and the one Truth behind all illusions.[1] Man, said Spare, ought to shed his dependency on his material security which enshrouds him in 'conventionality', and inquire instead beneath his 'mask' into his subconscious. This probing towards the macrocosm enabled man to realise his full potential. What man himself was, and what he could attain as an individual, Spare called ZOS.

His whole theory then hinges on the relationship between KIA, the Primal Energy, and ZOS, the human vehicle for receiving it. This was an inward, spiritual activity in Spare's view because he believed, as all mystics do, that the Godhead lay within. He was correspondingly dissatisfied with the world which lay without. Contemplating himself, he pondered on his own 'unreal self as humanity saw it', and came to the conclusion that he should follow the beckoning of the naked 'Primitive Woman', the Universal Mother of Nature, who could guide him pantheistically back to the Source.[2] This 'journey' which Spare describes is one within the psyche, and even in his earliest illustrated book he employs the effective device of giving symbols and ordinary depictions equal pictorial emphasis so that one is never quite sure what is 'real' in his drawings. The mystical quest is undertaken beyond 'the parapet of the subconscious' and this too is rendered as a literal circular pathway along which visionless old men dodder hopelessly looking to their candles for light, unaware of the 'Great Beyond'. People who are unable to rise above their material environment, says Spare, frequently take things on their face value; they are unable to perceive symbolic connotations. Spare shows us a depraved young man making lustful advances to the 'Universal Woman' in his failure to see beyond her enticing outward appearance. It is clearly a question of insight, for otherwise the wise, all-seeing Sophia of the Gnosis is mistaken for the Scarlet Woman of Babylon. Spare himself did not commit this error: "I strayed with her, into the path direct. Hail! the Jewel in the lotus!"

Mystics believe that Union with the Godhead is achieved when man is totally harmonised both within himself and externally with all things. It is the realisation that both macrocosm and microcosm are essentially the

---

[1] Spare defined KIA as "the absolute freedom which being free is mighty enough to be *reality* ..."
[2] In the Qabalah, the Sephirah or stage of consciousness, Malkuth, which corresponds to the visible Universe, is regarded as feminine. (The daughter of Kether, the first emanation). Robert Graves proposed that Nature is universally venerated, in various forms and guises, as the Great White Goddess.

same that shatters man's ego or insularity, and leads to the Great Liberation. So we find Spare saying "I myself am Heaven and Hell": in other words Austin Spare, in 1905 at least, was still an ego whose positive and negative qualities had not yet been reconciled or worked out. The process of harmonising these opposites in one's nature is a crucial one; Spare in his later work became highly aware of the need to overcome 'duality' in all its forms.

It is said, traditionally, that when one starts to evolve beyond the framework of the ego-centred personality, disillusionment may ensue because in the act of transcendence there is a tendency to become uprooted from humanity: correspondingly there is no longer any measure of achievement and no tangible gauge of 'progress'. Hence the term 'the black night of the mystic', when one feels cut off from the world and simultaneously unable to perceive any final meaning. It is only after a great period of mental anguish that the vision of the light of God begins to dawn within the minds of those worthy to perceive it. Spare talks of this: "The barrenness of this life but remains, yet in despair we begin to see true light. In weakness we can become strong. Revere the KIA and your mind will become tranquil."

In the same way that the purity of aspiration is its own judge, the mystical endeavour cannot afford to be mediocre. One must be thoroughly involved and not merely a dabbler. Spare is quick to point out that the 'normal' run of things frequently involves only a half-hearted commitment: most people give only part of their time to enacting their beliefs. He quotes as his text to the illustration 'The Inferno of the Normal', two verses from *Revelation* (Ch. 3: 15, 16):

"I know thy works,

That are neither cold nor hot:

I would thou wert cold or hot.

So then because thou are lukewarm,

And neither cold not hot,

I will spew thee out of my mouth ..."

This is illustrated by a drawing of a naked[1] youth standing above the parapet and drawing aside a curtain upon worldly chaos. Dishevelled

---

[1] Nakedness symbolises the 'recovered innocence' or 'purity': the state of Adam before the Fall.

bodies – the groping masses – are presented to view; these are the people who do not 'experience' but hide behind the curtain of Faith. Spare is entirely ruthless in his visual expressions, for his methods deal with self-realisation not self-trickery.

A well known concept in occultism involves the confrontation, on an inner plane of consciousness, with the so-called 'Dweller on the Threshold'. A vile creature, an embodiment of corruption, decay, vice, and sheer horror, it is none other than the accumulated self, the ego, presented to the onlooker as the anthropomorphic representation of his collected sin in incarnation. As a ghastly vision of one's 'karmic total' it has to be mentally overcome (first acknowledged, then transcended). It is not until this moment that the individual can reach beyond such degradation and realise the Divine nature behind his own appearance. And so it is that Spare comes to consider the Self as it really is: "We realise our insignificance to the incomprehensible intellect of the Absolute KIA (the Omniscient) and find out how subcutaneous our Attainments are!" Man has to ascend from the grime of the 'Dweller on the Threshold': the self has to undergo a purgative death and be spiritually reborn as Divine.

This level of attainment on the Qabalistic glyph, the 'Tree of Life', is represented by the sixth Sephirah, Tiphareth, an emanation which symbolises both spiritual renewal, and also all gods who are slain and rise again (Jesus, Osiris, etc.). In portrayal, Spare shows the skulls of lions lurking behind a disconsolate woman who is tied by chains to the feet of a cross on which the legs of a nailed body are just discernible. The title is 'Bodily Suffering, a resurrection of crime unpaid'; the theme is one of a Saviour figure (Christ) enduring and thus nullifying man's 'karmic debt'. This opens up the possibility that man may be rescued from the fate of a terrible death (symbolised by the skulls of lions); terrible because without the chance of rebirth or resurrection man's existence is totally and devastatingly meaningless.

Despite Austin Spare's acknowledgement of the Christ-attainment, however, he remained cynical about existing religious institutions.[1] These

---

[1] He was also critical of occultists who, like the Church, claimed to be carrying on a Tradition. This, Spare believed, led by its very nature to a loss of vitality. Kenneth Grant summarises Spare's attitude: "The ceremonial magician sets his stage for the rehearsal of reality with all the traditional weapons; but ZOS (Austin Spare) maintains that this is unnecessary mummery because the apprehension of our greater realities is to be effected consciously through living the symbolic simulations of the ego 'as if'

he called "obelisks of humanity's insignificance," projecting "incapacity, the imaginations of fear, the veneer of superstition ..." Not only was the Church too fundamentalist to transcend its own security in materialism, and its own ego; it was inherently unnecessary. For Spare believed that every human being, however 'degraded', is *essentially* Divine, although most failed to perceive it: "I have not yet seen a man who is not God already," declares Spare paradoxically. All man had to do was confront himself as he *really* was, and he would find God. Necessarily this involves the death of the ego, for it is the ego that insists we are distinct from other people and hence isolates us from the greater realisation of Unity. Spare therefore thought of death as a positive thing because it destroyed the pretence of personality: "From behind, Destiny works with Death. "And death, as we have indicated, is the precursor of enlightenment; Austin Spare presents us with a Qabalistic vision:

"... On entering at the Gates of Life,

Lo, I behold Knowledge the Jester.

Capsizing the Feast of Illusion,

The drawing aside false Truth.

He shewed us all –

The World,

The Flesh,

and

The Being.

This is the Alpha and Omega ..."

In the Qabalah, Kether diagrammatically represents the first emanation of God, the act of Creation 'out of nothing'. This is the highest level spiritual man can attain. [1] It is shown symbolically on the Tarot trump, corresponding to the Path leading to Kether, as the Jester or Fool. The reason for this seemingly absurd representation of the sacred is as follows: Kether is the point of First Creation and therefore total Non-Being

---

they were real, not a mock rehearsal but as a spontaneous evocation within the magical circle of immediacy – *now*." (*Carfax Monograph* IV.)

[1] This implies a God-like purity of being that few in history would seem to have attained; those who resist the dissolution into the Godhead and choose instead to stay to help mankind by imparting their wisdom are known as avatars. They assume Divine incarnations of the status of a Buddha or a Christ, for example.

precedes it. As a device which maintains the 'secrecy' of mystical symbols by making them outwardly nonsensical, the Jester is suitably chosen, for a fool is one who knows 'no-thing'. He is accordingly the wisest among all men for he has reached the highest possible state of consciousness. He has seen KIA, or negative existence. All of this involves a relatively orthodox Western mysticism, but Spare was already developing his own individualised philosophy, devoid of all dogma or 'belief '. He was steadily eliminating – or so he hoped – the 'vices' of "fear, faith ... science and the like," and was preparing for the plunge into his own unknown, his inner self.

With these ideas in mind, he came to write a book entitled *The Book of Pleasure (Self-Love):The Psychology of Ecstasy*, which first appeared in 1913.[1] In it were a number of important new concepts.

Now it is true that many occultists prior to this date had been emphasising the place of the 'will' in magical procedures. Florence Farr had outlined the need for intense mental concentration in her articles in *The Occult Review* (1908) and Aleister Crowley himself emphasised a form of mastery in "Do what thou wilt shall be the whole of the Law," by which he meant acting in accordance with the 'higher Will' or true nature. Austin Spare adopted this view too, but only up to a point: he then moved in a different direction.

Firstly Spare dealt with the methods of concentrating the will. Since the degree of effectiveness of any action is related to a thorough understanding of the command behind the action, Spare developed a way of condensing his will so that it was more readily grasped as a totality. He did this by writing his 'will' (desire) in sentence form, and by combining the basic letters, without repetition, into a pattern shape or 'sigil'. This could then be simplified and impressed upon the subconscious. Spare describes the process:

"Sigils are made by combining the letters of the alphabet simplified.

Illustration: the word 'Woman' in sigil form is:

---

[1] This had been preceded by *A Book of Satyrs* (c. 1911) which contained 'satires' on the Church, politics, officialdom, and other 'follies'. It is not a major work.

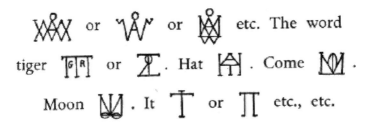

> The idea being to obtain a simple form which can be easily visualised at will ..."

What was to be done with the sigil once it was arrived at? And what was the significance of the sigil itself? We must first of all consider some related ideas.

As has been said before, Spare spoke of KIA as the Supreme Principle in the Universe: it was akin to a dynamic expanding Vortex of Energy, ever in a state of Becoming. Man was normally unaware of its full potential simply because he did not let it manifest in himself ("Are we not ever standing on our own volcano?"). Instead, he shut himself off by various 'insulating' devices employed by the ego. The only way in which the Energy *could* manifest (or be 'aroused' to use the metaphor applied to Kundalini) was by *thoroughly opening* oneself to it. It was when the individual was in a state of mental 'vacuity' (ultimate openness) that KIA became "sensitive to the subtle suggestion of the sigil." This state could be arrived at by emptying the mind of all its thought-forms in an effort to 'visualise' non-manifestation, e.g. 'blackness', 'emptiness'. In turn, this usually involved inducing meditation-leading-to-a-state-of-trance, in which the individual became oblivious of his surroundings as he focused only on the Inner Void. He would now be consciously attempting to transcend the physical, by eliminating its dominance of the senses. The contemplative state of mind, with its 'latencies', would become 'reality', rather than the earlier environment of the 'waking consciousness'.

Because we all proceed from the Godhead originally, argued Spare, it should be possible to trace back through the mind to its First Cause. Like most mystics, Spare believed in reincarnation and therefore he regarded the subconscious as the 'potential' source of all his own earlier physical embodiments or personalities, right back to the Beginning.[1] The psyche, as it were, consisted of a number of different 'layers' – the resulting impressions of successive lives, most of which were subconscious.[2] All of these were an aspect of the individual's own 'reality' (and ultimately everybody else's), in his own words:

"Know the subconscious to be an epitome of all experience and wisdom, past incarnations as men, animals, birds, vegetable life, etc: everything that has, and ever will, exist. Each being a stratum in the order of evolution. Naturally then, the lower we probe into these strata, the earlier will be the forms of life we arrive at: the last is the Almighty Simplicity."

Spare's intention was to gain knowledge of his concealed states, through 'regression', and eventually to lose his own self or individuality (ZOS) in the indescribably ecstatic Union with KIA, whose energy he had now come to consider to be basically sexual.[3]

The dark void of the mind, emptied of thought-forms through an act of concentration, could now be penetrated by the will by employing a sigil suitable for one's purpose. According to ability, one could, in theory at least, project the sigil to all possible recesses of the subconscious and hence gain access to the entire sphere of the imagination.

In reality this was harder to achieve than the theory suggests. Obviously it

---

[1] Spare believed that the self lived 'in millions of forms', and that it was obliged to experience 'every conceivable thing', i.e. all the infinite possibilities inherent in the manifested Universe. (They were also inherent in KIA but the self didn't realise that). Any incomplete existence or situation required a reincarnation to finalise it or make it whole: "I have incarnated that which I need to rationalise." Spare also thought that by exploring the inner recesses of the mind one would undoubtedly uncover past incarnations. "For whatever is attained is but a re-awakening of an earlier experience of the body."

[2] These 'impressions' contained a record of man's eternal past because they were aspects of the total Karma, the 'essence of self' which survived each separate existence. Spare soon realised that a great number of these subconscious contents were bestial and his later illustrations show an increasing intermingling between the *actual*, and these thought forms conjured up *in trance*. It is interesting to note that one of the methods employed by occultists is to identify with, and imagine oneself as, a God, e.g. Thoth. It is believed that in so doing, one experiences the qualities of the God and correspondingly one's own spiritual state is modified. The Golden Dawn and A.'. A.'. incorporated meditations on the Egyptian pantheon, and it is not surprising, in view of the fact that many of the Gods (Thoth, Horus, etc.) have animal heads, that some meditators should have acquired atavistic qualities. Crowley was keen to identify with the Great Beast 666 of *Revelation* and Spare frequently identified with the goat!

[3] Note Spare's reference to 'regression'. Most occultists and mystics prefer to consider their methods 'evolutionary'.

depends upon a number of crucial factors:

(1) The ability to derive a suitable sigil.[1]

(2) The ability to prevent random thought-forms from unintentionally disturbing the 'black void' and thus rendering 'impure' the individual's attempt to be a pure vehicle for the energies of KIA.

(3) The ability to reach further into the subconscious by totally renouncing the worldly grip on one's aspirations. Ultimately the task involved destroying the Ego, a most unworldly activity!

This last condition was the hardest to achieve. Spare says that 'total vacuity' is 'difficult' and 'unsafe' for those 'governed by morality, complexes, etc.', i.e. all the 'superstitions' and intellectual conceptions that man has surrounded himself with. Spare believed that to become totally receptive to the influx of Energy one would have to cast aside all contrived or finite rationalisations.

This state of being could be achieved by any discipline nullifying the ego or intellect, but in human terms it was hard, if not virtually impossible, to arrive at. Spare therefore tried to think of various situations where the rationale was minimal or absent. He tends to emphasise three such situations:

The first of these was the state of physical exhaustion. If one had a 'desire' or 'concentrated thought' in such a circumstance, Spare argued, the mind would become "worried, because of the non-fulfilment of such desire, and seek relief. By seizing this mind and *living*, the resultant vacuity would become sensitive to the subtle suggestion of the sigil." In other words, by exhausting the body one made it impossible for normal mental aspirations or commands to be carried out physically. The mind was therefore 'forced' into manifesting more transcendental concepts, embodied in this case in the sigil.[2]

Sheer exhaustion can be brought about in a number of ways, but a more notorious one in mystical circles is the sexual act itself. The Tantric technique of using orgasm as the 'leaping off ' point to visionary states of

---

[1] In order to attract at an inner level a 'true' response, the sigil had to be free of 'superfluous elements', hence its simplification. Otherwise uncalled for results could rebound from the subconscious.

[2] This method appears to resemble that of the Whirling Dervishes who induce visions by acts involving extreme physical exhaustion.

mind was well known at the time Spare was writing. It is probably also the basis of 'the vision of the Black Sabbath'. Aleister Crowley and Victor Neuberg, who had a homosexual relationship, employed it on a mountain in Algeria when they invoked into vision the entity Choronzon.[1]

The second method lay in exploiting the mental state of extreme disappointment, experienced, say, when one lost faith in a close friend, or when a cherished ideal had been destroyed: "When fundamental disappointment is experienced the symbol enshrining a quota of belief is destroyed. In some cases the individual is unable to survive the disillusionment. But if at such times the moment is *seized upon* and consciously experienced for its own sake, the vacuum attracts into itself the entire content of belief inherent in the person at the time of disappointment." Spare is saying, in effect, that when we thoroughly lose faith in a belief or ideal, we are given the option of transcending it, and transcendence of belief leads to ecstasy, as we are sucked into the vortex of KIA.

Both these methods involve rising above a symbol, 'leaping beyond the sigil', and 'destroying an Ego-ideal', respectively, so that the organic reality of KIA is allowed full expression in the human vehicle. Kenneth Grant notes that a most important idea of Austin Spare's was to allow desires implanted by sigils (at times when the ego was negated) to "germinate secretly and unobtrusively in the subconscious. "The desires would 'grow' in the seedbed of the mind until they became ripe and reached back down into the conscious mind. In this way one could manipulate one's own psychic 'reality'.

The desires incorporated in the sigils would eventually become moulded into the personality and the ego as such would be bypassed.

However, Austin Spare seems to have preferred a third approach, which in a sense implied the other two, and which could be used for both generalised changes in the personality and also specifics. This involved self-induced trance in which the body became rigid, ceased to function, and underwent what Spare called 'the Death Posture'. (This is similar to the second stage of Pranayama in Yoga, when after profuse perspiration the body as a whole becomes rigid. The third stage is a series of often quite painful spasms, described as 'jumping about like a frog', before the fourth

---

[1] See Jean Overton Fuller's *The Magical Dilemma of Victor Neuburg*, Allen, London, 1965.

and rarely attained stage of levitation). Spare describes a preliminary exercise designed to bring the Death Posture about.

Gazing at your reflection[1] (e.g. in a tall mirror) "till it is blurred and you know not the gazer, close your eyes and visualise. The light (always an X in curious evolutions) that is seen should be held onto, never letting go, till the effort is forgotten; this gives a feeling of immensity (which sees a small form), whose limit you cannot reach."

Spare considered that this exercise should be practised daily, and its results are more fully described in his next major book which was called *The Focus on Life* (1921).[2] But he had already alluded to the implications of the practice in an overall way.

"The Ego is swept up as a leaf in a fierce gale," he wrote, "In the fleetness of the indeterminable, that which is always about to happen, becomes its truth. Things that are self-evident are no longer obscure, as by his (i.e. Spare's) own will he pleases; know this at the negation of all faith by living it, the end of the duality of consciousness." Here Spare is alluding to the KIA Dimension, which is outside Time, but which is nevertheless the central basis of all potential. Finite occurrences are *latent* in the *un*manifest: when people 'open' themselves, certain aspects of the KIA can manifest. Pleasure for Spare was just this cosmic Realisation achieved by overcoming the dualities of the normal non- transcendent world.[3] For example he believed that he could transcend good and evil by rejecting the distinction, and he had a similar attitude to sex.

In summary his 'Death Posture' is, then, a procedure of conquering finite limitations. It seems to resemble, in effect, what other writers have called 'astral projection'.

This term unfortunately conjures up all sorts of pseudo-theosophical connotations. It refers nevertheless to the hazy, variable, ever-changing realm of the subconscious with all its sense impressions and memories. Occultists believe it is possible to wander consciously in this realm, through an act of 'projection' (will) which depends firstly on imagination. The general underlying theory is that each individual is a physical body

---

[1] This is a well known technique in 'astral projection'.

[2] Republished London, Askin, 1976.

[3] Spare wrote: "Man implies Woman. I transcend these by the Hermaphrodite, this again implies a Eunuch", i.e. Man / Woman in the world becomes the Hermaphrodite or Divine Union of the Sexes in Kether which in turn becomes the Eunuch or Non-Sex of Ain Soph / KIA.

animated by consciousness, and it is this consciousness which is the sole judge of reality. Because our physical body acts in a three-dimensional way in our waking consciousness, we tend to equate reality with the 'world of the senses'.

Now if it were possible to visualise, in the imagination, a simple shape, e.g. a sphere or a cube, and by an effort of will to transfer one's consciousness by auto-suggestion to it[1] so that one felt oneself to *be* the sphere or cube, to be 'in' it and to 'inhabit it', reality would then appear to be of the same quality as imagination was previously. 'Astral projection' is the passing into this very dimension, the creative psyche, the 'treasure house of images', through an act of determination. The importance of this procedure is discussed further in another chapter. One side effect, however, is that with the extreme degree of mental detachment from everything other than the projected mental image (the cube, etc.), the body becomes numb and the individual sinks into a deep trance. He may even appear dead, hence Spare's evocative label the 'Death Posture' itself.[2]

However, the Death Posture as a concept was, for him, much more than an act of mental fantasy; it was an act involving a confrontation between the microcosm and the macrocosm, the individual Self which Spare called ZOS,[3] and the KIA or the 'Atmospheric I', the Infinite Potential. It was a question of directing one's will into the cosmic memory and acquiring knowledge of earlier life-forms which were aspects of both oneself and KIA. The Death Posture provided the possibility of a link. The sigil confirmed the possibility. This brings us back to an earlier point where we departed at a tangent.

A sigil, as indicated, is a visual condensation of the will. However, what we 'will' can often be based on ideas of grandeur and self-deception. Spare points out that if we imagine ourselves to be great we are not so necessarily, and all the desiring in the world can't alter the fact. Spare notes: "Realisation is not by the mere utterance of words ... but by the living act ... The will, the desire, the belief, lived as inseparable, become realisation ..." Hoping for something won't help us achieve it; we must

---

[1] A similar technique to Tattwa visions in traditional magic.

[2] Occultists also believe that astral projection simulates the process of death. In the first instance the consciousness is projected into a vehicle forged by the imagination. In death the vehicle does not return, for the bond with the body is broken.

[3] The ZOS, according to Spare, needs to discover things about itself and KIA and this is the reason behind reincarnation, as explained earlier.

'live' it and enact it for it to become true.

In his own words Spare adds, "Belief to be true must be organic and subconscious. The idea to be great can only become organic (i.e. 'true') at the time of vacuity and by giving it form. When conscious of the sigil form (any time but the magical) it should be repressed, a deliberate striving to forget it; by this is it active and dominates at the subconscious period; its form nourishes and allows it to become attached to the sub-conscious and become organic; that accomplished is its reality and realisation. The individual becomes his concept of greatness." In summary, beliefs need to be 'organic' not theoretical in their origin; organic realities originate with KIA and lie dormant in the subconscious; we can use a sigil to embody our desire, command or will, and it may relate to what we want to do or become; the sigil can grow in the subconscious but will lose its effect if it is consciously remembered: the sigil will eventually manifest as a 'true' aspect of the personality since it comes from within.

Spare also relates this process to the faculty of creativity: "All geniuses have active subconsciousnesses and the less they are aware of the fact, the greater their accomplishments. The subconscious is exploited by desire reaching it. "This implies that geniuses not born, could be made.[1] He was not the only one to have this idea.

Now the sigils could embody transcendent commands affecting the whole body (ZOS) or they could relate to specific senses and abilities.[2]

Kenneth Grant, who knew Spare personally, tells of a situation where Spare needed to move a heavy load of timber without assistance. A sigil was required which involved great strength, so Spare constructed a suitable sentence: "This is my wish, to obtain the strength of a tiger." Sigilised this word would be:

---

[1] A theory often reiterated by Crowley.
[2] For example, said Spare, one would be able to hear within the mind "the most transcendental music ever conceived."

This my wish

To obtain

The strength of a Tiger

Combined as one Sigil or

Grant goes on to say: "Spare closed his eyes for a while and visualised a picture which symbolised a wish for the strength of tigers (i.e. the final sigil above). Almost immediately he sensed an inner response. He then felt a tremendous upsurge of energy sweep through his body. For a moment he felt like a sapling bent by the onslaught of a mighty wind. With a great effort of will, he steadied himself and directed the force to its proper object. A great calm descended and he found himself able to carry the load easily." (See Figure 12.)

Spare implied that no matter what method was used, one would arrive at 'the true sigil' for a given situation. This seems unlikely in view of the many different ways of expressing a desire. What is essentially most important, however, is that the individual is concretising his will by deriving a symbol for it that *seems* valid and therefore *is*. There is no question of whether Spare's method is 'more correct' than another: it appeared to work for him and was therefore pragmatically useful. A sigil will work for you if you believe in it.

Kenneth Grant makes it clear from his account that firstly dormant energy was awakened and then it was focused into a specialised activity. This was not always Spare's method, for in his more far-reaching 'atavistic resurgences' he allowed the influx of KIA to obsess him. His mind would become flooded with preternatural influences and there was no semblance of control. Spare relates how this in itself was an act of bravery: "Strike at the highest ... death is failure. Go where thou fearest not. Has canst thou be great among men? *Cast thyself forth!* ... Retrogress to the point where knowledge ceases in that Law becomes its own spontaneity and is freedom ... This is the new atavism I would teach: Demand of God equality – Usurp!"[1]

Thus the Death Posture, the first step, ultimately involves much more than mere transition. It involves the death of the Ego, an assault on the peak of Creation ('stealing the fire from Heaven'), and the utter negation of thought in supra-consciousness. But Spare at first found himself coming into contact with all sorts of forms and entities, and he came to see himself as a collection of consciousnesses many of which were bestial and hitherto unacknowledged ("This focus 'I', called consciousness, is unaware of its entire living embodiments"). Spare lets us share in his dreams, told in the third person:

> "The waters became murky then muddy, and movement began.[2] Going nearer he observed a phosphorescent morass crowded with restless abortions of humanity and creatures – like struggling mudworms aimless and blind: an immense swamp of dissatisfaction, a desire smashed to pieces. "This quagmire was soon none other than a vision of the 'degraded' human situation, the 'Inferno of the Normal', the terrible lethargy of inertia, that Spare himself was trying to overcome. The going was difficult, but he endeavoured to rise above it. "He was certain he had been there before by a staircase. But now there was no easy means of access. He would have to climb whatever served. After much painful effort he managed to reach and hang on to the balustrade of the upper floor. There he noticed innumerable strange effigies and new creations of humanity. He struggled further along to obtain an easy means of ingress ... when suddenly he observed another and more agile following him – who when reaching Aaos,[3] clutched hold of him – shouting, 'where I cannot reach, thou too shalt not ascend!', their combined weight became too heavy – the balustrading collapsed and they both fell ..."

---

[1] In his autobiography, Carl Jung warned against the possibility of allowing the symbolic contents of dreams and visions to be indulged in, rather than checked. Jung believed that the perception of dual, but intermingled, levels of awareness (e.g. atavism and reality) could lead to schizophrenia. One wonders if Spare would agree.

[2] In the illustration to this text, thought-forms swirl around a head which is undoubtedly *feminine*. In light of the fact that the book is titled *The Focus of Life* and contains Spare's own visions, this is rather puzzling. The other illustrations also contain naked (Primitive?) women, but no drawing of Spare himself, which is again unusual because in *The Starlit Mire*, Spare shows his own head surrounded by atavisms ('The Seven Devils'), and a similar drawing occurs in *The Book of Pleasure*. The only plausible reason for Spare's insistence on the feminine form in *The Focus of Life* is that it may refer to the occult doctrine of the alteration of the sexual polarity on successive mystical planes.

[3] A 'gnostified' extension of A.O.S., Spare's initials.

Spare was thus dragged back from transcendence by his lower 'normal' self which resisted both the destruction of 'security' and the vision of unsuspected archetypes at higher levels of awareness. But he was determined to indulge the 'pleasure' of Union with his Higher Self, which in *The Focus of Life* he describes in increasingly sexual terms: "Up! Up! My sexuality! and be a light unto all – that is in me." KIA is now 'the unmodified sexuality';[1] and Spare the open vessel for its uplifting energies.

Direct union with the awakened diverse forms of past incarnations, beyond which lay their ultimate focus, KIA, became his obsessive aim. Macrocosmically this aim constituted the Vision of the true Universal Identity; the indulgence in all the earlier shapes and outgoings of manifested experience. United in the pleasure of Self-Recognition, this would become the Final Liberation. The world of man, of morality, science and religious dogma could no longer claim him once he had achieved macrocosmic unity with the Primal Energy. He would pass *beyond experience*: "Abstinence from righteousness by total indiscrimination becomes limitlessness ..."

There remained, however, the problem of the Devil and the nature of Evil. In *The Focus of Life*, Spare describes a terrible dream: and dreams become significant because he has previously stated that "in future my dreams shall interpret themselves as will" (i.e. in reaction to earlier 'subconscious demands' through sigils). In this dream he visits an undertaker's apartment where he is shown his wife's dead body. The coffin meanwhile has just been constructed.

Spare is "given the choice of being burnt to death or buried alive with *her*! Naturally [he says] my choice was to be alone. But no such chance was to be mine ... I was buried alive with her corpse. With their [the undertaker's assistants] combined weight forcing on the lid. I thought I was dead, – for did I not hear the rushing winds? – when doubt crept into my soul. Then realisation of life dawned when I felt that cold corpse crushed against my body by the tightness of the coffin, – never have I realised such horror! With a mighty yell, my after-suspiration burst that overcrowded coffin into fragments. I arose thinking I was alone. But no, sitting by the corpse, amid the debris ... was the *Devil* grinning! To be alone and half alive with the Devil is not a welcome anti-climax ..."

---

[1] Aleister Crowley wrote: "When you have proved that God is merely a name for the sex instinct, it appears to me not far to the perception that the sex instinct is God ..."

"Then he spoke unto me: 'Coward! Where was thy courage? ... Ah! ah! Thou hast indeed willed power. Thou or I? What medicine for the dead Gods! Thou wretched scum of Littleness – heal thy gaping wounds, thou art more fitted to pray than prey.'" ... Spare evidently succeeded in 'willing away' the Devil but he was obsessed with further doubts: "Perhaps," he says, "I became the Devil?" ...

We shall never know the answer of course, but the situation is reminiscent of one in which Aleister Crowley once found himself. He had reached a state of consciousness where he said of himself that: "I was in the death struggle with self: God and Satan fought for my soul ... God conquered – now I have only one doubt left – which of the twain was God?"[1]

Our only other clue to the workings of Spare's mind and its achievements rests in his evocative drawings, which are superbly executed and often depict in detail the 'atavistic resurgences' which Spare himself conjured up. The fact that they contain bestial elements in no way brands Spare as a diabolist because his method, as we have seen, involved 'regression' rather than the more orthodox 'evolution'.

"The Law of Evolution," says Spare, "is retrogression of function government progression of attainment, i.e. the more wonderful our attainments are, *the lower in the scale of Life the function that governs them*. Man is *complex*, and to progress, must become simplified." Because more and more manifestations of KIA are appearing all the time through reincarnation, as the Source of Creation expands 'outwards', the 'true' direction is 'inwards' or *'backwards'* to the First Cause.

The magnificent illustrations in *The Book of Pleasure (Self-Love)*, which were drawn between 1909 and 1912, show an atavistic merging of forms. One of these, entitled 'The Ascension of the Ego from Ecstasy to Ecstasy'[2], portrays Spare as a winged head (consciousness) rising above the Naked Primitive Woman, then merging with an ibex shape which eventually becomes a deer skull. One plausible interpretation of this important drawing could be: Mother Nature is the door to the Greater Reality which can be found only by penetrating things as they appear. The earlier animalian (and other) incarnations can then be explored subconsciously until the Ego finds its first point of existence and then finally 'dies' in the

---

[1] John Symonds, *The Great Beast*, Rider, London, 1952, p. 11.
[2] A.O. Spare. *The Book of Pleasure (Self-Love)*. London, 1913, p.7.

absorption within the KIA.[1]

We will offer no final judgement on Austin Spare's way of thinking since it is uniquely phrased, and allows no immediate comparison with other schools within the occult tradition. It is quite another thing to say that, as a method, it has far-reaching implications and appears to work. It is therefore immensely significant.

We conclude with a few characteristic sayings from the man himself:

> "He who subordinates animal instincts to reason quickly loses control ... control is by leaving things to work their own salvation."

> "Only when there is no fear in any form is there realisation of identity with reality."

> "We are what we desire ... Desire nothing and there is nothing that you shall not realise."

> "Revere the KIA and your Mind will become TRANQUIL."

Finally, may peace be with Austin Spare and his 'atavistic resurgences' ...

---

[1] Spare once referred to the soul as consisting of 'the ancestral animals'.

Figure 10: 'Forces of the Sigils' – painting by Austin Osman Spare
(reproduced from the collection of Jimmy Page, with the owner's permission)

Figure 11: Magical Stele: 'Formula of Zos vel Thanatos' – painting by Austin Osman Spare.

Figure 12: 'Elemental Manifestations' – painting by Austin Osman Spare.
(reproduced from the collection of Jimmy Page, with the owner's permission)

II

BELLADONNA

"The Witches who were Magicians as well as Devil worshippers apparently shared the magical and pagan sense of the value of the animal side of human nature. Dancing and revelling in animal costumes and the orgiastic worship of an animal god imply the letting loose of the animal in man. In magical theory, this is an essential step to the achievement of wholeness, in which a man becomes divine."

— Richard Cavendish, *The Black Arts*

The Devil has been described as "a large black monstrous apparition with horns on his head, cloven hooves, ass' ears, hair, claws, fiery eyes, terrible teeth, an immense phallus, and a sulphurous smell ..."This was the Horned God of the Witches, who was sometimes a goat, sometimes a horse or stag, and who provided a demoniac challenge to the Church from the 12th century onwards. It was He who was believed to incarnate in the coven leader, who in turn imitated the guise of the Devil by appearing to his fellow witches in a horned mask and in animal skins smeared with oily substances. Such gatherings were to become the subject of intense persecution throughout Western Europe specifically because their blasphemous ceremonies were regarded as a direct, pagan mockery of the Christian religion. We quote a contemporary account of what ensued at the Witches Sabbath:

> '"When all the wizards and witches arrive at the place of rendezvous, the infernal ceremonies begin. Satan, having assumed his favourite shape of a large he-goat, with a face in front, and another in his haunches, takes a seat upon the throne; and all present in succession pay their respects to him and kiss him on his face behind. This done, he appoints a master of the ceremonies, in company with whom he makes a personal examination of all the witches, to see whether they have the secret mark about them by which they are stamped as the Devil's own. The mark is always insensible to pain. Those who have not yet been marked receive the mark from the master of ceremonies – the Devil, at the same time, bestowing nicknames upon them. This done, they all begin to sing and dance in a most furious manner, until someone arrives who was anxious to be admitted into the Society. They are then silent for a while until the new-comer has denied his salvation, kissed the Devil, spat upon the Bible, and sworn allegiance to him in all things. They then begin dancing again with all their might, and singing ... In the course of an hour or two, they generally become wearied of this violent exercise, and then they all sit down and recount all their evil deeds since last meeting. Those who have not been malicious and mischievous enough towards their fellow creatures receive personal chastisement from Satan himself, who flogs them with thorns and scorpions until they are covered with blood, and unable to sit or stand. When this ceremony is concluded, they are all amused by a dance of toads.

Thousands of these creatures spring out of the earth, and standing upon their hind legs, dance while the Devil plays the bagpipes or the trumpet. These toads are all endowed with the faculty of speech, and entreat the witches there to reward them with the flesh of unbaptised infants for their exertions to give them pleasure. The witches promise compliance. The Devil bids them remember to keep their word, and then, stamping his foot, causes all the toads to sink into the earth in an instant. The place thus being cleared, preparations are made for the banquet, where all manner of disgusting things are served and greedily devoured by the demons and witches – although the latter were sometimes regaled with choice meats and expensive wines, from golden plates and crystal goblets; but they are never thus favoured unless they have done an extraordinary number of evil deeds since the last period of meeting. After the feast, they begin dancing, but such as have no relish for any more exercise in that way amuse themselves by mocking the holy sacrament of baptism. For this purpose, the toads are again called and sprinkled with filthy water, the Devil making the sign of the cross and the witches calling out oaths. When the Devil wishes to be particularly amused, he makes the witches strip off their clothes and dance before him, each with a cat tied round her neck and an other dangling from her body in the form of a tail ..."[1]

The most important witch gatherings during the year took place on May Eve, 30 April (known in Germany as *Walpurgis Nacht*), and on All Hallows' Eve, 31 October. Prior to meeting on these occasions the witches would rub their naked bodies with magical ointments, mount upon their broomsticks, and fly from their windows or chimneys into the night sky. Or so legend has it. At the culmination of the Sabbath described above, they would engage in orgiastic revelry, transform themselves into frolicking animals, and copulate with the Devil. These activities ceased at cock-crow as darkness began to dissolve in the oncoming light of day.

Witchcraft has a strong sexual undercurrent as is shown in the testimonies of Anne Marie de Georgel and Catherine Delort who spoke of erotic extravagances with the Devil, and that of Jeanette d'Abadie who suffered painful intercourse with him. However, there seems also to have been a notable hallucinatory element. Antoine Rose, a witch tried in Savoy in

---

[1] Quoted in *The Occult Review*, Vol. 9, 1909. See Figure 13.

1477, stated at her trial that she had made use of certain ointments which, from her account, produced both psychic and sexual enhancement. The Devil, she said, had given her a stick 18 inches long and a jar containing ointment which was to be smeared upon it. She placed the stick between her legs exclaiming "Go, in the Devil's name go!", and in so doing rode through the air to the Sabbath. In light of the Devil's supposedly remarkable sexual powers it seems impossible to conclude, as Pennethorne Hughes does, that the broomstick is "a symbol of woman." It is clearly the male phallus, whereby the witch 'flies' into her demoniac ecstasy. In this statement, furthermore, reference is made to special ointments which enable the witch to *fly through the air* to the Sabbath. Hughes thinks that aerial travel is a metaphor applied to witches as they scurry rapidly over the ground. It seems more likely that the potions contained hallucinogens which caused a sensation of weightlessness, and which, coupled with ecstatic orgasm, gave rise to the witches' idea of having travelled a long distance and made love with a god. This implies that the Sabbaths were in one sense literal; they were meeting places where witches engaged in orgiastic excesses – but they were also, in another sense, transcendent, diabolical psychic 'happenings' prone to exaggerations of the imagination.

Is there any evidence that witches' ointments contained such activating qualities? Professor H.S. Clark thinks there is. Writing in an appendix to Professor Margaret Murray's book *Witchcraft in Western Europe*, he stated that some concoctions which were used at Sabbaths did have toxic qualities which could provide a sensation of flying through the air as in a dream. "Hemlock and aconite," he concludes, "would produce mental confusion, impaired movement, irregular action of the heart, dizziness and shortness of breath." In a second ointment, the belladonna used "would produce excitement which might pass into delirium" and a mixture containing belladonna and aconite together would induce "excitement and irregular action of the heart ..."

It has been suggested that the hard, broken skin of witches would enable such ointments rubbed in deep to enter the bloodstream through cracks and scores. This in fact seems highly plausible. But it might also be possible that witches made use of techniques resembling those of the Tantrics, Eastern exponents of Sex Yoga. A passage in the *Malleus Maleficarum* says that the Devil "can prevent the flow of the semen to the members in which is the motive power, by as it were closing the seminal duct so that the semen does not descend to the genital vessels" (II, Ch. ii). In sex rituals, the Tantric yogi through an act of will withholds the ejaculation of semen to allow his (and his partner's) ecstatic vision to extend in climax for longer than normal.

Was the Devil, as manifested in the medieval coven leader, similarly able to extend the sexual climax, thus enabling hallucinating witches to transcend the physical nature of their intercourse? Were the witches using sexual energy as a catalyst to assist in gaining the Vision of the Horned God ...?

Another striking feature of the witch-cult was the belief that wizards and witches could turn themselves into animals at will. This practice, known as *lycanthropy*, caused considerable fear among the local inhabitants of witch infested hamlets. Pennethorne Hughes relates a 16th century case from Auvergne where a gentleman who was out hunting was suddenly attacked by a monstrous wolf which was immune to bullets. In the struggle the hunter lopped off the creature's forepaw and placed it hurriedly in his pocket as he escaped for his life. He later produced his trophy to show to a friend but discovered to his amazement that he held not a paw but a woman's hand with a wedding ring upon one of its fingers. The friend recognised the ring as belonging to his wife and ran home to find that she now had a bloody stump where her hand should have been. The woman was subsequently burnt publicly as a witch, before a very large crowd.

Another case is mentioned in Adolphe D'Assier's *Posthumous Humanity*:

> "A miller named Bigot had some reputation for sorcery. One day when his wife rose very early to go and wash some linen not very far from the house, he tried to dissuade her repeating to her several times, 'Do not go there, you will be frightened.'
>
> 'Why should I be frightened?' answered she.
>
> 'I tell you, you will be frightened ...'
>
> She made nothing of the threats and departed. Hardly had she taken her place at the wash-tub before she saw an animal moving here and there about her. As it was not yet daylight, she could not clearly make out its form, but she thought it was some kind of dog. Annoyed by these goings and comings and not being able to scare it away, she threw at it her wooden clothes beater, which struck it in

the eye. The animal immediately disappeared. At the same moment, the children of Bigot heard the latter utter a cry of pain from his bed and add, 'Ah! the wretch, she has destroyed my eye!' From that day, in fact, he became one-eyed. Several persons told me this fact, and I have heard it from Bigot's children themselves."

Dr. Hereward Carrington, the psychical researcher, writing in *The Occult Review* (Vol. 9, 1909), has suggested that lycanthropy refers to a situation where an individual is able to project his consciousness so that it "adopts a non-human vehicle imaginatively created or that it dominates by will the body of a real animal. Injuries to such a body would transfer back to the body of the source consciousness."[1] In the case of Bigot, then, the animal shape was none other than his projected consciousness, or astral double.

As a hypothesis this could also apply to those cases where witches who are known to have stayed in their rooms have sunk into trances and on waking have reported vivid details of what ensued at the Sabbath.

---

[1] The theory, practice and implications of 'astral projection' will be discussed in a later chapter, but the reader is also referred back to the section on Austin Spare.

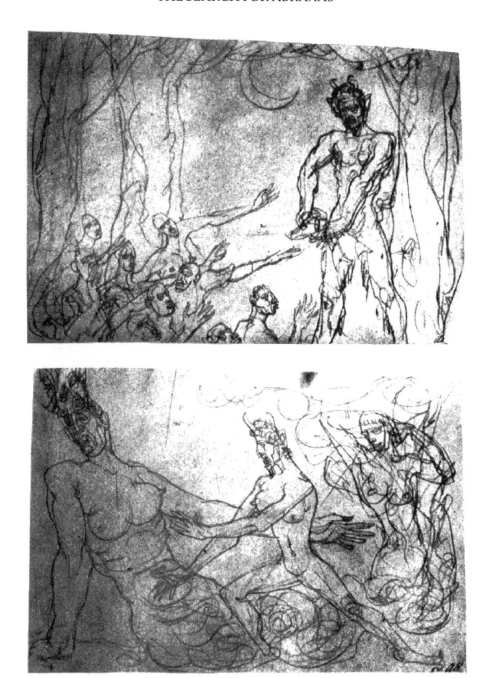

Figure 13: 'The Sabbath' – drawings by Austin Osman Spare.

III

LOS DIABLEROS

The belief that witches can transform themselves into animals is not found only in Europe. It is a widely held notion, for example, in Meso-America, surviving even in present times as a remnant of a Pre-Columbian witch tradition originally held in honour of Tlatzolteol, the great Earth Goddess who was supposed to assist in producing fine harvests of the hallucinatory drug peyote. Tlatzolteol is depicted on talismans riding naked upon a broomstick and is sometimes accompanied by an owl ...

In modern-day Guatemala and Mexico, the Aztec-derived word 'nagual' is commonly used in connection with belief in witch-transformation although it tends to mean different things, and varies in spelling, from place to place. The Nahuatl of Tepoztlan, for example, use 'nagual' to describe any person, male or female, who is capable of turning himself into an animal, usually a dog or a pig, and the Tzeltal and Tzotzil Indians of Chiapas employ a related term 'nawales' to describe the animal counterparts – dog, horse or mountain lion – which a man may assume supernaturally to gain power for himself.

However, Benson Saler, an anthropologist who has studied the phenomenon in depth, has indicated that 'nagual' and its variants often denote a second self or double, which is not always animalian but can also resemble the wind or a comet. This implies a spirit nature. "Should the *alter ego* suffer harm," he says, "It is widely believed the individual whose destiny is linked to it (i.e. the animal form) is likely to suffer harm in a corresponding degree."[1] In other words, should the projected vehicle containing the witch's consciousness be impaired, the witch will suffer bodily and mental harm as a result. This concept resembles closely the medieval witch tradition in Europe.

The Quiché Indians of Santiago El Palmar in Guatemala more specifically differentiate the term 'nagual', which means in their usage the *affinity* that a witch has with an animal, from the term 'win', the actual practitioner. Some of the Quiche believe that the nagual is related to the characteristics of the person, that is to say, a witch with a tiger nagual would be brave and savage. Others consider the nagual to be the creature of the astrological sign one is born under, on the basis that the date of birth in some degree predetermines one's character. The 'win' on the other hand is

---

[1] Benson Saler, 'Nagual, Witch and Sorcerer in a Quiche Village' in *Magic, Witchcraft and Curing*, edited by John Middleton, American Museum Sourcebooks in Anthropology, p. 71.

THE SEARCH FOR ABRAXAS

the witch himself, the lecherous nocturnal prowler who in his animal body prays to the Devil in the cemetery, steals from his neighbours, and rapes unsuspecting women in their sleep.[1] Normally, the win assumes bird or dog-like form but he can be recognised instantly by his movements which are always unnatural and contrary to the manner of the species. He is frequently hideously ugly, with red glaring eyes, and he makes a habit of choosing virtuous people for his victims. Luckily, the animal-spectre of the win can be halted in its tracks by the continued recital of "Our Father ..."

Another category of evil-doers is distinguished by the Quiche and these are the 'ajitz' or sorcerers, who do not derive their power from the Devil as the win does, but from magical formulas and rites.[2] Unlike the win the sorcerer usually chooses specific victims whereas the win is in an overall sense malevolent and a threat to all who crosses his path. Some sorcerers engage in relatively minor operations, like burying artefacts belonging to the intended victim in the hope that both will decay, but many others are credited, like the win, with the ability to transform into phantasy or real-life animals for evil purposes.

In 1960 an American anthropologist student named Carlos Castaneda was visiting the Southwest for information on how Indians use medicinal herbs. He was introduced to a Yaqui Indian called Don Juan who came from Sonora, Mexico, and had a reputation for using certain hallucinogenic plants, including peyote, to achieve magical effects. Don Juan was at first reluctant to part with his 'secretos' but after an initiatory period he accepted Castaneda as an apprentice in sorcery. The timeless and often terrifying visions which Devil's Weed ('la yerba diablo'), peyote and the psilocybe mushrooms bring about became a new reality.

Castaneda was taught certain things which are normally connected with the witchcraft tradition and which hardly seem feasible in the present day. One of these was the rubbing of magical unguents into the skin. Don Juan showed his pupil how to prepare an odiferous paste from the root of the datura plant (Devil's Weed) which according to legend had been used by Indian 'diableros' to transform themselves into animals for evil purposes. This concoction induced the soaring, aerial effect so often reported by

---

[1] According to the Quiche, the witch attacks the opposite sex only, and so this statement would not apply to female witches.
[2] Informants told Benson Saler that some sorcerers had learnt these rites from "the magical books of the Jews." Is it possible that the Qabalah has reached the Quiche magicians?

medieval witches at their trials. Castaneda says: "I looked down and saw Don Juan sitting below me, way below me … I saw the dark sky above me and the clouds going by me … My speed was extraordinary …" He felt as if he no longer had a body and was capable of changing into anything; there could be no limitations. Don Juan suggested that he should learn to fly properly by "becoming a crow."[1]

In Don Juan's opinion mushroom-smoke was more satisfactory than Devil's Weed as a means of achieving this transformation. Having indulged in the 'little smoke' ('humito') Castaneda focused upon a creation of his imagination and it immediately became real. His head, guardian of the consciousness, metamorphosed so that it became a crow: legs emerged from his chin, a tail from his neck, and wings from his cheeks. A beak extended between his eyes and he now saw laterally instead of straight ahead. At Don Juan's command he was able to fly confidently, and his Universe was instantly ablaze with radiant lights and colours.[2]

Thus we have an insight into what sorcerers may have performed in the past. The consciousness was projected into the realm of the imagination and in so doing conferred upon it a sense of reality. In this way we believe we can account for all witches and 'diableros' who were, and are, supposedly able to transform themselves into animal bodies. It might also be possible, as Dr. Hereward Carrington has suggested, to mentally dominate the 'will' of an animal and enter into its body causing distinct changes in its behaviour.

Transformation phenomena, as has been seen, are a thing of the present as well as the past, although perhaps they are less practised today. Don Juan says: "I think we have lost interest and now power does not matter any more." One thing we do know, however, is that the practice is at least as old as Ancient Egypt, home of Magic and the man-animal deities. We quote the following witch account from Lucian:

"The woman first undressed herself, and going to a lamp threw two

---

[1] Don Juan wanted Castaneda to adopt not only a suitable, but a 'safe' form. Crows, he said, were usually ignored by other birds and so nothing much could go wrong. It would be unwise however to choose any creature sought as prey: crickets, lizards, etc. Don Juan may have been thinking that if another sorcerer were to inhabit a 'superior' vehicle he could inflict harm upon Castaneda while in the animal body, thus endangering his very essence.

[2] Castaneda (1925-1998) was savagely debunked in the 1970s, and accused of making it all up in order to get his Ph.D, but this does not detract from the many valid insights into both magic and psychoactive drugs which are to be found in his books.

grains of incense into the flame and recited certain words; she then went to a large chest containing several bottles, and taking out one which contained oil, rubbed all her body with the liquid, from head to foot, beginning with the ends of the nails, and suddenly feathers and wings began to grow upon her, and a hooked, horny beak took the place of her nose. In a very short time she resembled a bird in every respect, and when she saw that she was well feathered, she flew upwards and, uttering the cry of a night-raven disappeared through the window ..."[1]

---

[1] Sir Wallis Budge, *Egyptian Magic*, University Books, pp. 204-205.

Section III
The World of Dreams

Some twenty-four centuries ago, Chuang Tzu dreamt he was
a butterfly, and when he awoke he was not sure whether
he was a man who had dreamt he was a butterfly
or a butterfly who now dreamt he was a man.

I

PHANTASY IN ART

The Victorians were a proud society, for they had fulfilled a dream. They had built an Empire unequalled in history, they had brought many 'pagan' nations under the sway of enlightened British culture and they had raised the standard of living at home to a new peak, or so their statistics said.

There was a technological boom, more machines, finer buildings, and it was undoubtedly an age of progress. Material progress. For the Victorian was inclined to measure progress in terms of wealth. And Great Britain, with all her productive colonies, was a wealthy country now.

All of this amounted to a kind of smugness whereby prosperity itself acquired a certain virtue, and perhaps even beauty. The ugliness which industry and the inequality of wealth produced was not specifically forgotten, but it was repressed because it was unpleasant.

It was towards the end of the Victorian era that a certain artistic gentleman considered that society's short comings should be exposed graphically. His name was Aubrey Beardsley and his illustrations were preposterous. Fat leering society women reared on the wealth of the land stared forth from his drawings as the epitome of moral degradation. Ladies who should have known better worshipped giant phalluses, and aristocrats blithely whipped their servants or indulged in decadent perversities behind jewel-encrusted doors. A type of rot was exposed. Beardsley believed that his satires were a corrective. The vision of evil had to be laid bare before the smug upper class which had repressed its social and sexual extravagances beneath a veneer of respectability.

But Beardsley was only the first of a number of dedicated artists and illustrators who felt obliged to maintain the vision of corruption. The intricate decorative details, the splendid use of black, grey and white values based on lines and dots to accommodate the new printing processes, all of these were to be continued in a school of illustration which might best be described as 'Late Art-Nouveau, Decadent'. Many names spring to mind, some of whom were perpetuators of Beardsley's vision of evil. Others merely copied his line techniques and extended them into new phantasies which have been revived in contemporary psychedelic art. Among the figureheads of the 'Decadent' school were men like Harry Clarke, Alastair and John Austen. Of Harry Clarke's life little is readily ascertainable except that he died at the premature age of 41, and his best work was done in the 1920s. His version of *Faust* with its demoniac embellishments is perhaps the most potent vision of darkness since Hieronymus Bosch's Hell scene in 'The Garden of Delights'. (See Figure 16.)

Published in 1925 in a limited edition of 1,000 copies, Clarke's illustrated *Faust* throngs with grotesque animal shapes, bodiless eyes, and semi-human concoctions of various sorts, a veritable quagmire of the subconscious. His characters have theatrical, stylised poses which imply a sense of ritual drama, and they invariably look out upon the world with melancholy eyes as if they are beholding truths far more intolerable than mere man can endure. Clarke's other masterpiece is Poe's *Tales of Mystery and Imagination* (1920) which is filled with organic curiosities, distorted bodies and sordid death scenes – in general a pantheon of sheer horror, although his illustration to '*Morella*' does have a beautiful dream quality. (See Figure 15.) Like Beardsley, even Clarke's sinister vision contains a transcendental element. It lifts man to a stage where he discovers, and must acknowledge, his other half, the section of his personality which corresponds to his psychoses, repressions and cumulated vice, the obverse of his respectability. Clarke continued what Beardsley was doing, only he penetrated much deeper into what we really are.

The artist Alastair, whose real name was Hans Voight, was a German from Munich who lived in magnificent isolation in a 17th century Bavarian hunting lodge. An actor at heart, he was also fond of music and dancing, and his drawing, which is baroque and decadent in style, shows tendencies which resemble those of a great fashion designer of the times, Erté. Alastair, who had no technical training in art but who perfected his own style nevertheless, also followed Beardsley as Clarke had done. However, the Victorian decay which inflamed Beardsley was not so intense for the European, who has correspondingly contributed relatively few grotesque or satirical pieces. His 'Demon' (from Wilde's *Salome*) and 'Herod' (from Flaubert's *Temptation of Saint Anthony*)[1] are perceptive creations in this vein though, the latter depicting the evil inherent in power. Alastair contributed drawings for books and periodicals from the splendid obscurity of his home from 1914 onwards, and like Harry Clarke, his personality remains hidden behind his work. He did produce some vignettes for *The Golden Hind*, which has already been mentioned in connection with Austin Spare who was its editor, but probably his most

---

[1] Contained in *Fifty Drawings*, published by Knopf in New York, 1925. See Figure 17 and Figure 18.

impressive work is contained in Oscar Wilde's *The Sphinx*, and in *Fifty Drawings*. Like Clarke, Alastair often gives his characters rigid theatrical stances but communicates a vast range of emotion particularly through the rendering of the eyes. They reflect a vision of things seen but unproclaimed; a latent horror hides beneath the baroque frenzy of the linework. Alastair's characters invariably look strained and sad as if they have pity both upon those who cannot penetrate appearances, and upon themselves who cannot endure the insight.

John Austen, the English illustrator who also followed in the wake of Beardsley, combines these same qualities with an emphasis, too, on the sexual extravagances of Victorian eroticism. Naked decadent ladies flaunt their form in much the same way as Beardsley's do, but their openness is their revealed ugliness. Austen's most distinctive work from our point of view was done before 1925. After this date he moved in directions which owed little to his original sources, and his drawings began to resemble stylised woodcuts.

In summary, the 'Decadent' school of illustration achieves its synthesis by visually correcting human deficiencies. These deficiencies are presented as the things about ourselves which we would rather forget but which we must come to grips with if we are to 'know ourselves'. And self-knowledge implies recognition of the 'evil' side of our nature.

A parallel school in British illustration which presented the essence of the supernatural as opposed to the 'normal' but through much more gentle contrasts, included men like Arthur Rackham, Edmund Dulac (see Figure 21) and Danish born Kay Nielsen. Their ethereal watercolours of fairy elementals and nature spirits have never been equalled, and they contain much that mirrors Tolkien in our own time. Rather than present evil as the vital but repressed component of man's nature, they strove to lift the senses into something purer, more serene, eternal. The phantasies of these men, who became famous for their goblins and mythical heroes, are sublime and unsullied by a social context. It is little wonder therefore that these drawings appealed mostly to children who did not yet know what society and 'life' were about. There is almost nothing 'real' about *Rip Van Winkle*, *The Tempest* or *Hans Christian Andersen's Fairy Tales*, for in an illustrational sense, these are adventures of the spirit.. And therefore they are invaluable, for apart from being delightful as art they ultimately point the way to a new dignity.

Now while these developments were being enacted mostly in England, a phantasy school of quite a different order was evolving on the Continent. This was an attempt to lift man above himself; this too offered man a Universe enlarged by greater realisation. Its name was Surrealism.

Figure 14: 'Silence' – by Harry Clarke.

Figure 15: 'Morella' – by Harry Clarke.

Figure 16: Illustration from *Faust* –by Harry Clarke.

Figure 17: 'Herod' – Alastair (Hans Voight)

Figure 18: 'Demon' – Alastair (Hans Voight).

II

SURREALISM

"We lay no claim to changing anything in men's errors but we intend to show them the fragility of their thoughts and on what shifting foundations, what hollow ground, they have built their shaking houses."

— *Declaration du 27 Janvier 1925*

As a movement, Surrealism was not, as Roger Shattuck has recently suggested, "highly disciplined and tightly organised." It consisted in fact of many diverse and curious activities whose sole common purpose was to manifest the irrational and mysterious. Many strange actors were involved in this drama, among them Yves Tanguy who ate live spiders, Robert Desnos who went continually into trances, Philippe Soupault who used to ring doorbells at random asking "if Philippe Soupault did not live there," and Wolfgang Paalen who pondered the mysteries of the seventeenth Tarot card, 'The Star'.

Surrealism of course involved much more than mere eccentricity. Announced in Paris, and flowering between the two World Wars at a time when many people felt alienated from society, Surrealism was an attempt to find new perspectives. Logic, tradition and 'normality' were utterly renounced; phantasy took their place. Maurice Nadeau has said that Surrealism "was never a doctrine but an attitude of mind" and Patrick Valdberg has called the endeavour not a 'formal movement' but a 'spiritual orientation', although Dali with his phallic preoccupations and Miro with his sexual phantasms were not specifically mystical in their inclinations. There was, however, a turning towards the subconscious as the potent vortex of imagination, which led in turn to an adoration of visionaries, alchemists, occultists, and mediums, as penetrators of this relatively uncharted realm.

Founder figures André Breton and Philippe Soupault meanwhile investigated automatic writing, whereby one endeavours to write so fast that there is no logical control. This precipitates transcendental elements which Breton believed involved the 'dictation of thought' without the restraint of the mind. More important, however, as a means of access to the Great Mystery, was the interpretation of dreams. In the First Surrealist Manifesto of 1924, Breton, as mouthpiece of the movement, explained why he believed in 'the omnipotence of the dream'. Dreams, he thought, were not only a reflection of life, but ultimately a more valid visual representation of reality, because their forms were unimpeded by rational processes. Having studied Freud at length, Breton longed for the day when dreams would be methodically analysed as a continuing sequence, for he saw them as an everlasting inner commentary upon man's finite dimension. Breton considered that the combination of dream with reality produced a much more meaningful Universe, "a sort of absolute reality, a

THE SEARCH FOR ABRAXAS

*Sur*reality."

It is the pursuit of this 'Surreality' that links in essence the styles and techniques of many otherwise dissimilar artists, some of whom employed loose abstract forms, and others who painted with meticulous care for detail.

In the first category we find, for example, Wolfgang Paalen, the Austrian artist who lived for a time in Mexico and invented a technique known as 'Fumage'. Paalen would hold canvases freshly coated with oil paint above a candle so that the smoke would trace random patterns in the wet paint. These suggested shapes would then be used as the basis of an abstract supranormal composition. 'Conflict of the Principles of Darkness' is one such picture (see Figure 19). We observe also Wifredo Lam with his hypnotic shapes and André Masson, medium for dynamic undisciplined forms, among many other artists of this type.

In the naturalistic category can be included René Magritte and Salvador Dali, both of whom transpose ordinary, everyday objects into alien contexts; Yves Tanguy who depicted superbly detailed phantasy structures; and Paul Delvaux who peopled his classical Greek backgrounds with naked women entranced as if in a dream, but painted in an entirely representational manner.

We discover the great eclectic, Max Ernst, lurking somewhere between the two extremes, fluctuating, as it were, between the poles of different techniques; drifting from the emergent bird and animal shapes in 'Alice's Friends' to the atavistic realism of 'The Robing of the Bride' (see Figure 20). Ernst also invented a process which, like Breton's automatic writing, provided an entry into the subconscious. This was a technique known as frottage.

Ernst would rub lightly with pencil upon sheets of paper placed upon his floorboards, thus allowing the uneven surface to come through on his paper as a texture. He then manipulated his newly discovered textures by filling in areas where the grain ran in different directions, thus arriving at a simple picture. But when Ernst looked carefully at his frottages he found that he was able to perceive things latent within them which he had not suspected were there: "When gazing at these drawings," he writes, "I was surprised at the sudden intensification of my visionary faculties and at the hallucinatory succession of contradictory images being superimposed on each other ..."[1]

We therefore find Ernst using these creations as 'leaping-off points' into visionary states, in much the same way as Austin Spare had used sigils. In fact Spare anticipated the Surrealists, both in his philosophy and application, by at least 10 years.

In the First Surrealist Manifesto Breton had stated: "A work cannot be considered surrealist, unless the artist strains to reach the total psychological scope *of which consciousness is only a small part* ... There prevails at this unfathomable depth a total *absence of contradiction* ... a *timelessness*, and a substitution of psychic reality for external reality all subject to the *principle of pleasure* alone ..." Is this not exactly what Spare had stated in his later writings and incorporated into his drawings?[2]

Elsewhere Breton writes: "Surrealism will introduce you to death which is a secret society. It will glove your hand entombing there the consummate 'M' with which the word Memory begins." Does this not refer to the initiatory state which Spare called the Death Posture, and which provided access to the hidden memories and images within the subconscious?

In the early years Breton had observed that in wartime man found his relationship to the despoiled world to be valueless and intolerable. Would this realisation lead them to a new Revolution, a search for meaning whereby all archaic and traditional concepts were cast aside and new transcendental values adopted in their place? Breton certainly hoped so. Colleague Paul Eluard spoke of this Revolution as equating with "*real* life, like love, dazzling at every moment ..." Regrettably post-war society has hardly heeded the message. Although there are recent signs of change, it has remained, on the whole, embedded in materialism and as pragmatic as ever.

We would suggest that perhaps in the final analysis Surrealism remains valuable not as the precursor of an age of instant enlightenment, but rather as a gauge of human consciousness in terms of art. The artists involved in the movement were all reaching further and further into the hidden recesses of the mind, and their paintings can be seen as indicators of the psychic levels attained. This can hardly be avoided, for the mystical

---

[1] Quoted from Patrick Waldberg, *Surrealism*, Thames and Hudson, London, 1966, p. 97.
[2] The italics in this quotation have been inserted to demonstrate the remarkable parallel between Austin Spare and the Surrealists.

journey produces archetypal visions common to all who travel the path. The temperament and personality of the beholder merely fashion the way in which the vision is perceived.

We have already seen that the Qabalistic 'Tree of Life' is a symbolic glyph depicting various stages of the visionary quest. Now although the Qabalah in itself is profoundly Jewish, the archetypal psychic levels which it describes are independent of any specific culture. Indeed the parallels in religious symbolism which are found in both ancient and modern independent pantheons exist because the same fundamental realities have been experienced in the first place: "The Gods do not die, only their names are changed ..."[1] Thus we can use the 'Tree of Life' to charter levels within the psyche even in modern times.

Until recently the inner experience was almost exclusively the domain of mysticism and religion. But with the break away from 'realism' in art at the beginning of the 20th century, and the contemporary rise of psychology and psychoanalysis, experiences hitherto regarded as sacred have begun to filter into secular circles. The Surrealists themselves were not specifically 'religious'. But the essence of their work was undoubtedly transcendental as has been already indicated.

According to our hypothesis it ought then to be possible to estimate the Surrealist attainment, using the 'Tree of Life' as a guide. The vision experienced within each Sephirah has as its characteristics certain symbols, colours and motifs. We would expect the Surrealists to mirror these in their work.

The tenth and final Sephirah Malkuth relates to the manifested Universe as we perceive it and so all acts of transcendence begin here. René Magritte, the Belgian Surrealist, shows a respect for 'reality' but he nevertheless twists it out of its normal perspectives. Gravity fails to operate in his pictures. In 'The Castle of the Pyrenees' (1959) we are shown a massive boulder floating above the ocean waves in a state of precarious levitation. In another composition an extraordinary meteoric body consisting of a lion, a tuba, an armchair, a sewing machine, and a Graeco-Roman sculpture, wafts through the atmosphere oblivious of the demands of the natural order. Magritte also 'overcomes' reality by presenting physical

---

[1] M.W. Blackden, 'The Wisdom of the Mysteries in Egypt' in *The Occult Review*, Vol. 5, 1907, p. 310.

images in combinations which defy normal classification. A mermaid with the head of a fish and the legs of a woman lies hopelessly cast up upon a beach; a succulent green apple fills a room; and plants which are also birds grow profusely upon a rocky mountain-top. Magritte undoubtedly derives his inspiration from the visual Universe, but he exposes the limits of three-dimensionality and indicates at the same time that we may proceed beyond.

Yves Tanguy, a more mystical Surrealist, joins us at this point. During the late 1920s,Tanguy was producing some remarkable oil paintings which superficially resemble underwater scenes, yet at the same time exude a peculiarly ethereal effect: curious half-forms float limply in an alien atmosphere of dusky grey, and a feeling of inner space is implied, unlike anything with which we are commonly familiar. 'With my Shadow' (1928) and 'The Lovers' (1929) are works of this type. Throughout his career Tanguy retained his subdued colours but he later populated his dream dimension with unusual mechanical structures held together in impossible harmonies by fine threads. Finally his 'Multiplication of the Arcs' (1954) sees a return to dull earth and granite 'skies' of supernatural grey.

There is something unmistakably lunar about Tanguy's landscapes. In addition, his mechanical structures, which are never quite real, seem always to be prototypes for something eventually more definite and more recognisable. Tanguy seems to have been preoccupied with a state of consciousness known by Qabalists as Yesod, which is one phase removed from Malkuth, the sphere of the Earth. Yesod is ruled by the Moon, its colours in visions are sombre greys and purples and it is the first level of the astral within the subconscious. In terms of creative emanations proceeding from the supernals, the twilight shapes of Yesod represent a state of 'potential' structure always about to become fully manifest in Malkuth below.

Because Surrealists Magritte and Tanguy remained 'true to form' it is relatively easy to correlate their work with the specific Qabalistic Sephiroth which dominate. Other artists within the school were more variable and their sources of inspiration fluctuated. Max Ernst's late work, for example, is characterised by solar motifs which are linked Qabalistically with Tiphareth, the sphere straight above Yesod and Malkuth on the 'Middle Pillar'. These symbols had already occurred fleetingly in a sequence painted by him in the 1930s under the title of 'The

Entire City', which showed stark mottled ruins beneath a dominant Sun, as sole provider of energy in a dying world. But more recently the orb has re-emerged as a motif in 'The Dark Gods' (1957) and in an important series of grandiose backdrops for a modern ballet. In addition to his 'Solar' work Ernst has also contributed a notable series of paintings ('The Nymph Echo', etc.) in which Nature is presented in its most chaotic aspects. Prompted by the horrors of the Second World War, which threatened to engulf Nature in a mechanical hell, these pictures equate with the Sephirah Netzach which symbolises organic growth and whose colour is green.

A number of other Surrealists would seem to have uncovered varying degrees of degradation and evil in the subconscious and in view of earlier comments on the 'Dweller on the Threshold' this does not appear surprising. In the Qabalah, such demoniac aspects are called Qliphoth and they are the shadows of the Sephiroth. Felix Labisse's macabre women with insect heads, Victor Brauner's ego-taunting devils, and the obscurely evil landscapes of occultists Kurt Seligmann and Wolfgang Paalen, reflect these tendencies.

An exhaustive study of all the Surrealist modes would obviously fill many volumes and cannot be attempted in a short space here, but it does seem plausible that the paintings described above are indeed the result of inspiration derived from various subconscious levels.

We suggest that the whole Phantasy movement of the Decadents and the Surrealists was an attempt by a number of artist-magicians to overcome material limitations and to probe the recesses of the mind for an Inner Reality. In doing so they uncovered many remarkable aspects, some of which were spiritual and others demoniac, some mystical, others atavistic. For these men were the explorers of duality, the polar opposites within the psyche. They have passed on to us the visions which were their adventures.

In so far as they were searching for greater meaning they too pursued the Gnosis to which we have been alluding. They too, were searchers for Abraxas.

Figure 19: 'Conflict of the Principles of Darkness' – Wolfgang Paalen.

Figure 20: 'The Robing of the Bride' – Max Ernst.

III

ASTRAL PROJECTION, DEATH AND THE INNER VISION

The Surrealists drew their inspiration from the subconscious, the world of dreams: the one 'mystical' experience common to all of us, since everyone dreams. Dreams are no less a mystical experience than a willed and worked-for contact with the subconscious; they are the spontaneous expressions of our subconscious selves, albeit distorted by a censor who deforms our memory of them upon waking, into an acceptable form. Dreams are, as the psychoanalysts have found out, one of the easiest egresses into the subconscious. However, because this state is experienced every night of our lives, even if we forget we have dreamed, it has come to be regarded as commonplace, as a distraction to be wondered at next morning.

We have seen how Austin Spare projected his thought-sigils into his subconscious while in the Death Posture, how Don Juan taught Carlos Castaneda to transfer his being into the imagined form of a crow, and how the Surrealists and 'Decadents' attempted to merge subliminal images into a greater Reality. All of these men climbed, as it were, into their dreams; they penetrated the very origins of thought, the potent, creative vortexes within their psyche. The 'magical act' occurs when one becomes one's idea. In so doing the entire frame of reference is changed because consciousness is no longer restricted to a finite context. The projected self now encounters images and symbols, no longer subjective but real. And because the act of mental exploration is a conscious one, three-dimensionality is still perceived as coexistent with the 'living dream'. In one's barren room, hitherto inhabited by oneself only, might be found lurking a mythological gryphon, a sinister grotesque which has escaped from one of Bosch's paintings, or some aspect of the divided self which one had not realised was capable of separate anthropomorphic existence!

These creatures are *real* on the astral plane, just as solid three-dimensionality is 'real' on the physical plane. As we know that matter exhibits wavelike characteristics, and that atoms are mostly space: perhaps the atomic nuclei, so stubbornly substantial, are only compacted waves of another order of existence.

In occult terminology astral forms *can* exist coextensively with the physical objects of the room. In fact the old idea of 'ghosts' being able to pass through walls is a 'folk awareness' of this law of the astral plane. Likewise the astral body can pass beyond the walls of a house as easily as it passed beyond the walls of the body.

The phenomenon which we have been discussing, and which is termed by Western occultists 'astral projection', indicates that what occurs in the imagination is as real to the psyche as the messages of the senses perceived in normal consciousness. Two main disciplines are involved. The first is the ability to imagine and sustain within the mind a simple three-dimensional shape which is to all appearances 'real', already mentioned as the first necessary skill of an aspirant in the West. The second prerequisite is the ability to transfer one's entire consciousness to the created mental image so that it becomes one's new 'body' or 'vehicle' on the astral plane.

Before launching into techniques for astral projection it is important to reiterate that the magical philosophy posits four 'bodies' or *modes of consciousness*. These are the physical, etheric, astral, and mental bodies.

The physical body is a conglomeration of cells and atoms built up from the intake of the four Elements, in the form of food (Earth), drink (Water), oxygen (Air), and light (Fire) which are formed into the characteristic shape of the individual by an etheric mould. Now, as it is well known, the cells that make up the body are in a state of flux, that is, they are generated and they die, but the new cells follow the same pattern, although this pattern weakens as it ages, or as it is subjected to greater than normal stresses such as a debauched life might impose on it. The pattern or energy field that determines the shape of the physical body occasionally breaks down and a wild profusion of uncontrolled cell growth breaks out, commonly called cancer.

This etheric body which forms the physical is in turn affected by the astral and mental bodies, thus making the physical body a rough reflection of the type of being inhabiting it. Further, part of the etheric body can be separated from the physical body with advanced forms of projection, under anaesthetics (where the pain messages of the physical body cannot reach the mental body, as there is no connecting etheric matter) and under some forms of hypnotism. At death the etheric body separates completely and the organisation of the body's cellular structure immediately begins to break down, and the chemical processes of decomposition take over from the etheric-directed process of cell building. The etheric is thus the 'matrix' of the physical body.

The third body, the astral body, is much more 'plastic' than the etheric, just as it in turn is less rigid than the physical. It draws for its substance on the directed imagination. It is this body which is formed by the mind into a vehicle for nocturnal excursions, be it unwittingly in dreams, of which only disconnected memories are brought back, or in deliberate astral projection in which the 'Body of Light' is formed as a vehicle for consciousness beyond the physical body.

Before commencing the actual work of building this vehicle, it is wise to perform the Banishing Ritual of the Lesser Pentagram which has the dual purpose of clearing the air of any distracting influences and concentrating the attention on the magical work in hand. A third reason is to ensure that the body is protected from any undue external influence whilst the astral is projected.

Then, suitably comfortable in a dimly lit room upon a couch or in *asana*, an image of oneself should be built up, so that it becomes solid and apparent to the inner eye in all its details. This image can be simplified by viewing it as a hooded and robed figure but seen as definitely being oneself. The image should be seen as coinciding with the physical body and seated or lying in the same position. When this is firmly visualised it should be gradually moved away from the physical body, till it is some distance from it. The aspirant should then perform mentally an exercise known as 'the exercise of the interwoven light'[1] in order to make the experimenter more conscious of each of his three non-physical bodies. If the 'exercise of the interwoven light' can be pictured as taking place in the space occupied by the visualised body or simulacrum, this will have the effect of transferring some of the matter of these three bodies to it.

Now it is necessary to put the simulacrum through its paces by willing it to stand up, sit down, walk around and so on. An extension of this exercise is to visualise the simulacrum going through the actions of the Banishing Ritual of the Lesser Pentagram, which, if thoroughly learnt by the experimenter, will help to identify the experimenter with his simulacrum.

If at any time during this phase one begins to feel as if the banishing is being conducted by oneself, not the simulacrum, this is the moment in which to identify with *its* point of view, to see from *its* direction; to be aware of a body lying at some distance upon a couch, which after a few seconds' thought is seen to be one's sleeping physical body.

Once having achieved this switch of consciousness, which is marked by an

[1] See W. E. Butler, *The Magician, his Training and Work*, Aquarian Press, London, 1963, pp. 94-99.

unmistakable click which is heard inside the head, one has to continue to exert effort to remain *out* of the body, rather than, as commonly feared, worry about getting back in.

Usually, astral projection will only be achieved after many abortive attempts and can be likened to a knack, which is hard to explain or achieve but once found, with a little practice, is easily duplicated at will. Just as a child gets used to controlling its body as it grows up, so the experimenter will find his astral body more easily manipulated, more able to go longer distances from the physical body, and able to stay out for longer periods of time, the more it is used.

One of the first signs of success in astral travel is a feeling of rocking slowly backwards and forwards as if at the end of a long pendulum; this is in effect the loosening of the astral body. During one's first astral projection it is usual to find that apart from a strange sense of disorientation, there is a coolness in the limbs (of the astral body) and a feeling of being able to float, although the latter takes some concentration to control efficiently. There is sometimes a feeling like a hand pressing one's solar plexus which is where the link with the physical body connects with the astral form, but this lessens as the astral body grows stronger. One disconcerting thing about the condition is that as in dreams (which are similar in that they occur on the same plane) thinking of something strongly is enough to instantaneously bring it within one's immediate range of perception. Thus one can leave the room by merely imagining oneself outside it. At first only the physical objects of the room are apparent, although they seem illuminated by a bluish glow, but if one allows oneself to concentrate upon ideas other than the immediate surroundings the scene tends to fade and be replaced by a 'dream sequence' of images.

For quite some time, however, investigation of the physical surroundings in the astral body is quite enough to handle without reaching out to levels of the astral of a more subjective nature. For example, it is worthwhile practising visiting familiar surroundings, remembering details and checking up on these later, if only as a personal proof of the reality of the phenomena.

Other levels of the astral can be reached by visualising the astral body as rising rapidly and simultaneously picturing the desired destination or portal symbol. The images can be ordered by using the signs and symbols attributed to various parts of the Tree of Life to direct one's progression through these realms. Thus one might commence, for example, at Malkuth and have the choice of three Paths, these having being accessible by using the Tarot trumps, The Moon, Judgement or The World, as a door which would lead respectively to the Spheres of Netzach, Hod or Yesod.

The anthropomorphised ideas and feelings which will be encountered here will be similar to those described in an earlier chapter on skrying, with the difference that whilst in the astral body apparent 'reality' will be more pronounced.

Returning to the body is a process which must be done as slowly and with as much care as leaving it, for although there is an ever-increasing pull trying to snap one back into the body, it is wise not to yield to it. One should carry out *all* the operations of leaving the body in *reverse* order. Thus, if the 'trip' had included the passing through of symbolic portals, each one passed should be returned through until Malkuth is reached, and one is standing in the astral body near the physical body. Then the *consciousness* should be transferred to the physical body, so that it wakes to perceive the now empty Body of Light standing in front of it. This should then be willed to move into the same spatial area as the body and an effort is made to reabsorb it, at the same time asserting mentally the Unity of all three 'bodies'. If this is performed faithfully, not only will the projection of the astral body be easier next time, as the thoughtform of the Body of Light has already been built up, but also the thoughtform, *if neglected*, can be indirectly a hazard to the experimenter, as it may be taken over by other entities.

Normally, much of the experience gained during astral projection will be remembered like that of a dream, for in fact astral projection is a very special form of dreaming, so it is desirable to have some way of recording it directly. This can be done, after facility in astral travelling has been secured, by concentrating on the physical body in such a way as to activate either hand or voice. Like Phillippe Soupault and André Breton, who investigated automatic writing as an aid to communicating the contents of the subconscious, so automatic writing (if one has already been accustomed to it) can be used whilst one is astrally projected to communicate one's experiences. Alternatively, the voice can be concentrated upon so that the physical body enunciates the thoughts of the consciousness which is at the time focused in the astral body. These faculties, however, are as difficult to achieve as the initial projection.

There is a further step beyond astral projection that can be taken, but only after a great facility in the control of the astral body is attained.

This step is etheric projection. To accomplish this one must first project the astral body, and whilst watching the physical body, imagine that a white cloudlike replica of the body is being drawn out of it. One then strives to unite with this form, and if successful, there will be a marked change in the breathing rhythm of the physical body. As the breathing of the physical body becomes irregular, one should commence to breathe *in the astral body*. As the astral takes up the burden of breathing the physical body will lapse into a state resembling a cataleptic trance, its breathing will cease and the body will take on the appearance of death. When the breathing in the astral body ceases, then the etheric matter will return to the physical body, which will revert from a trance state to that of sleep.

Whilst the etheric body is withdrawn from its physical envelope by 'astral breathing' the *prana* which is normally absorbed by the physical body is now being transmitted via the extended etheric body. Connecting the physical body with its extended etheric body is a tenuous cord of etheric matter, often referred to by occultists as the 'silver cord'. If this is broken at any time the death of the physical body, apparently from heart failure, will ensue. Consequently, it is *most important* that the physical body be secured from any possibility of disturbance during this operation.

In most magical usage, *astral* projection should be adequate, but where it is essential that a more 'material' vehicle be used, then *etheric* projection may be employed, providing adequate safeguards to protect the physical body from disturbance are observed.

Astral projection is significant because it implies that man's consciousness can exist actively as an entity free of the physical organism. The 'astral double' in fact equates with the concept of the soul (in the sense of Nephesh) as the component which survives the death of the body,[1] the latter being seen not as the originator of consciousness so much as its outward vestment.

If it is true to say that our dreams are vivid reflections of both what we are subconsciously and what we have actually experienced, and that we enter

---

[1] The Nephesh also disintegrates after a while, leaving the Spirit free.

a type of dream-state, or astral Universe, when we die, it becomes clear why mystery schools advise their initiates on both visionary revelation and the anticipated after-death imagery. In the latter instance the person involved lacks a material reference, he has no body. There is no dichotomy of 'real and unreal' to guide him. He is immersed in all the anthropomorphic embodiments of his own emotions. He must know how to react. Are these projected images real? They seem to be and yet the mystery traditions are consistent in stating that in the final sense such images are 'maya', illusion, and not to be heeded. For if the individual takes the visionary contents on their face value, be they god-like or demoniac, he is confusing the symbol with the indescribable Infinite Reality that they reflect. Accordingly, both the man who surrounds himself with angels thinking he is in Heaven, and the man who is unable to shrug off the terrible appearance of devils thinking he is doomed to Hell – both these men fall short of the true Nirvana which is Boundless in all respects, and without specific form or attributes.

As religious concepts, Heaven and Hell thus acquire new meaning. They are not locations as the superstitious believe, but mental states. [1] Nevertheless, they are every bit as real to the disembodied psyche as the physical dimension is to the senses. Our virtues and vices are presented to us as Gods and Demons.

Our destiny is resolved by whether we choose to pursue the positive, harmonising aspects or the negative, divisive qualities inherent in our own being. And in *our* being is the essence of *all* Being. Or as the Gnosis says: "As above, so below."

The *Bardo Thodol*, or *Tibetan Book of the Dead* as it is known in its English translation, is a manual which deals with the varying stages of consciousness encountered by man outside his physical body. Carl Jung, who wrote an introduction to the English edition, considered that the book was intended as a guide to after-death experiences, thus preparing the dying for what was about to happen to them. It is true, in fact, that passages from the *Bardo Thodol* are used in last rites by Tibetan priests for this very purpose. Jung's viewpoint has been criticised by Dr. Timothy Leary who believes that the *Tibetan Book of the Dead* deals primarily with initiation; the death of the ego and the rebirth of the Spirit. This process,

---

[1] See also J.B. Cabell, *Jurgen, A Comedy of Justice*, Crown Publishers, New York, Chapters XL-XLIX.

essentially transcendental and 'other-worldly', reminds man of his Divine origin, so often forgotten in the 'Sangsaric' world of normality.

Surely both men are right. For there seem to be clear parallels between the after-death experience and the projection, under will, of the 'astral double'. In one instance the 'double' does not return to the body, in the other it does. But both processes involve self-realisation, the essence of initiation.

Tibetan Buddhists believe strongly in the principle of Karma, or reaping the fruits of one's own deeds. The reincarnation of the self through different bodies and experiences provides the lessons by which the individual gradually comes to re-acknowledge his Divine Source.[1] This realisation lifts him away from material considerations and further 'rebirth', through initiation or reincarnation, becomes unnecessary. It is not a crucial issue whether the mystic receives his revelations in a transcendental, visionary state or whether he is finally united with the Godhead in the after-death dream by aspiring to the deity-projections of his own mind.[2] To acquire such knowledge may take a few incarnations or it may take many. For the Buddhist, the concept of time is of little importance: we are, after all, going to the same place. We will all get there eventually. It is up to us to decide our pace.

---

[1] As a doctrine, Reincarnation is not to be taken lightly. Not only is it the only after-death hypothesis which has any chance of empirical verification, but a considerable amount of evidence in favour of it exists already. Perhaps most important is the work of Dr. Ian Stevenson, the American medical scientist who is at present involved in research on very young children with vivid memory patterns far beyond the scope of their present lives. The children's information is verified against historical records; some statements involving place descriptions have proved to be true only in the distant past because changes have more recently occurred in the named locale. Such information would be inaccessible to the often illiterate and untravelled children who have these memories. Stevenson's work has been presented in his 1961 award-winning William James Lecture, and in his book *Twenty Cases Suggestive of Reincarnation* (American Society for Psychical Research, 1966).

[2] Another type of evidence is that compiled by hypnotherapist Arnall Bloxham, who employs hypnotic techniques to lift his patients into their 'past lives'. These people frequently undergo extreme personality changes and any utterances made under hypnosis are recorded on tape. These statements are then checked for indications of historical validity, often involving painstaking and difficult research. In some instances information known only to a very few specialists has been uncovered hypnotically, and it is this that makes Bloxham's research all the more extraordinary.

Figure 21: 'Ariel Attacks' – Edmund Dulac.

Section IV
The Search for Abraxas

"The bird is struggling out of the egg,
The egg is the world,
Whoever wants to be born must first destroy a world.
The bird is flying to God.
The name of the God is called ABRAXAS."

— Hermann Hesse

CONCLUSION

The Search for Abraxas is a search for Reality: from time immemorial man has realised that he has only perceived a portion of 'reality', and over the ages techniques have been formulated for the cognition of other phases of existence.

The ancients expressed this search in terms of Initiation into the Mysteries, Christianity in terms of the acceptance of Christ, the mystic in terms of Union with the Godhead, and so on. Even modern philosophy acknowledges that the senses are a very limited organ for the perception of reality. Sinclair has proved to his satisfaction that 'reality' is screened by a censor (not Freud's censor) which admits only that amount of experience which man is capable of handling.

Science extends our fields of knowledge using instruments such as the telescope or the microscope to extend the range of perceptions of our senses, but occultism, in its search for the greater realities beyond man's senses, uses techniques which, although not always as apparent as those of science, are in some cases as precise and in most cases less well understood.

Pursuing this line of thought, reality as a whole can be experienced by expanding the limits of the censor. In the phraseology of occultism this is called 'opening the third eye' or 'initiation'; in the case of chemically activated illumination, it is known as 'going on a trip' (although these are not necessarily the same). There has always been a wide selection of paths by which man has tried to get beyond thought to another mode of cognition, call it what you will, super-consciousness, transcendence or initiation. During the last decade, as also in the late 19th and early 20th centuries, there has been a great upsurge of interest in the occult and the paths available have increased in number. With the aid of science, which has produced L.S.D., synthesised mescaline and isolated a number of 'utopiate' alkaloids, modern man has again been made aware of the techniques of consciousness expansion. The upsurge in attempts to expand consciousness is not merely a reaction to the arrival of a greater number of means of so doing, but a reaction by the subconscious to the increasingly materialistic attitude of nations whose leaders see the 'Great Society' purely in terms of material prosperity. The result of the 'psychedelic revolution' in particular have been a return to the countryside, to the tilling of the soil and the living of a simpler, less hurried life, manifesting greater awareness of the forces of Nature and the elements.

Each Path has its price however; for the Yogi it is the agonising control of his body before he can focus his mind on the Ultimate; for the Magician it is the possibility of being ensnared in the symbols which are used to bridge reality and falling into the illusion that they *are* reality. If drugs are used, then it is not drug dependence in the normal sense that is to be feared (for the major psychedelics are *not* addictive) but the failure to make the connection between drug experiences and ordinary life. It is the retreat into the wealth of sense-symbol-expressions as pleasurable experiences, instead of using them to structure consciousness and life, that must be avoided.

There is the added hazard of interpreting the welter of perceptions and visions as real: they are only real in the sense that each phase of consciousness is closer to the Ultimate Reality. As yet, these levels have been relatively uncharted by the explorers of 'inner space'.

This upsurge in availability, interest in, and use of psychedelic drugs has sparked off an instinctive return to occultism in an effort to disentangle the mazes of subconscious material finding expression through these drugs, or to explain their particular illumination in terms of the illuminations of other men of other times.

Here we begin to see an application of the keys which have been found applicable to man (as modelled in the mystery tradition), fitting into locks which have been formed recently by the advances of science. Science, however, although it has discovered L.S.D., does not have the key to using it. The Qabalah is one such key, possibly the most reliable one, as it is the Western psyche, both individual and collective, which is being influenced by the new psychedelics, resulting in changes both individual and social.

If this proves to be correct, it reinforces the view that the Qabalah extends its validity to *all* corners of the psyche of man; even those 'opened' centuries *after* the Qabalah was first set down in writing. Of course, these new 'openings' are old ones, that the Qabalah had experienced not through drugs, but through hard work, devotion and that indefinite quality, inspiration.

In any system of illumination one must be aware of relative truth or relative reality. It is 'true' to the man in the street that magic doesn't exist; it is 'true' to the would-be initiate that magic does exist. However, to the initiated, 'magic' does *not* exist, inasmuch as the effects described by this word are the result of application of exact formulae and laws which have not as yet found their way into the canon of accepted science.

Each of the above three statements is true to the person concerned, likewise the laws applying to each plane are different and often contradictory: on the physical plane two objects cannot occupy the same space at the same time or travel sufficiently fast for the same object to be in two places at the same time. However, these occurrences are quite in order in terms of the laws of the astral plane. To apply the laws of one plane to the other results in inaccuracy and confusion.

Confusion of an intermediate plane or a relative truth with an ultimate truth, is merely an exchange of one illusion for another; thus, the indiscriminate use of drugs has provided a number of unstable personalities with a new *apparent* reality upon which to exercise their unstable egos, proclaiming to whoever will listen that 'they have found reality'. This is not to deny that drugs can play a part in exploring other areas of consciousness normally not accessible, but merely to point out that usage of anything as drastic as a psychedelic drug without some idea where one is going,[1] or even where one has been, is going to leave the aspirant with whatever neurosis he started with, distorted into a frame of reference with which he is even less familiar: in short a flight from reality.

The solution to this apparently endless progression of planes is to use an already established 'Uranography[2] of the mind' which will enable one to explore consciousness systematically and determine a direction in which to evolve.

Similarly in the Western Tradition, it is not simply a matter of invoking or evoking a series of gods, demons, spirits, or angels, but its practice must consist of systematic reawakening of those extensions of consciousness that for most of us appear to have been closed for ever by our civilisation or upbringing. With the aid of such a Uranography one can determine one's weaknesses and correct them.

This becomes very relevant when considering techniques for expanding

---

[1] In the sense of exploring the *inner space* of one's mind.

[2] Uranography literally means 'star chart', for as Aleister Crowley has said, "Every man and woman is a star," referring to their inner Selves. Thomas Fuller in *Pisgah-sight of Palestine*, 1650, Book v, p. 189, says: "Perusing the nine last chapters of Ezekiel's prophecy, whilst I hoped to find ... a literal sense, I found the Canaan by him described (to be) no Geography, but *Ouranography*."

consciousness which have no systematic background; such as the psychedelic movement. Timothy Leary has provided it with an *Eastern* background by adapting the *Tibetan Book of the Dead*, which categorises a 'trip' into three phases: First Bardo or period of ego-loss and non-game ecstasy; Second Bardo, or period of hallucinations, from archetypal forms, through wave constitution-of-matter visions to Creator visions; and the Third Bardo of 're-entry' or return to non-Bardo consciousness.[1]

However, since it is the Western mind, with its own archetypes, that is undergoing the 'psychedelic experience' it is more appropriate to apply a Western charter of the psyche. It is for this reason that we have dealt in this book primarily with traditions closer to home, and specifically one that is highly applicable in our own time, the Qabalah. The Golden Dawn brought together the strands of esoteric Jewish teaching, Rosicrucianism and the Mystery Religions and forged them into magical and mystical ceremonial which expanded the consciousness of its participants through initiation. The times in which this occurred were characterised by rampant materialism, similar to that which has produced, as an effect, the total rejection of many values inherent in the corrupted American Dream of today.

One of the most significant after-effects of the Hippie movement has been that many young people have experienced profoundly significant religious insights and are currently searching for a philosophy or teaching which adequately explains the 'realities' previously apparent under drugs. The so-called Jesus Freaks, as clergyman John Bisango put it, "are turning on to Jesus." However, the majority of latter-day Hippies remain unable to enter a world dominated by faith. For the drug experience breeds an enquiring approach. Firstly, visions; but then one wants to know just what is going on. It is therefore hardly surprising that the new approach is primarily non-institutional, pantheistic, eclectic, and theosophic. The truth is sought in *The Bible* perhaps, but also in the *I Ching*, in Professor Tolkien's mythology, in the mystical writings of Hermann Hesse, in the Tarot cards, in the UFO literature, in the Qabalah ...

It is as if we have lost sight of something which has to be regained. As if, perhaps, we have been ignoring that other side of ourselves, our *potential*.

---

[1] A Bardo is a level of consciousness or after death state, in the Tibetan system. For details of Leary's adaptation, see T. Leary, *The Psychedelic Experience*, University Books, New York, 1964.

This is why the current search for inner knowledge or Gnosis involves a *synthesis*. All facets of life have to be accounted for, whether good or evil, for otherwise the imbalance weighs heavily and the memory of the bad trip remains.

There is an animal in man, and there is a God in man. In order to produce a harmonised microcosm these aspects of our nature have to be firstly acknowledged: it is then that the self may be transformed. Perhaps the God which best symbolises this mystical venture is the one who is both a man and a hawk; He who is of the Sun and whose legs are coiling serpents, symbol of Wisdom reaching down to Earth. He who holds the sacred shield ... and whose name is *Abraxas*.

Figure 22: 'Night Flower' – Nevill Drury.

BIBLIOGRAPHY

SECTION I: *The World of Light*

I

Blavatsky, H.P. *The Key to Theosophy*. Theosophy Company, Bombay, 1931.

_____ *The Secret Doctrine*. Theosophical Publishing House, Adyar and Madras, 1962.

Chaplin, J.P. *Rumor, Fear and the Madness of Crowds*. Ballantine Books, New York, 1959.

Newbrough, J. *Oahspe, A Kosmon Bible*. London and Sydney, 1926.

II

Allen, P.M. *A Christian Rosenkreutz Anthology* (incorporating the writings of Heinrich Khunrath, Robert Fludd, Thomas Vaughan, Henricus Madathanus, Rudolph Steiner and others). Rudolph Steiner Publications, New York, 1968.

Bouisson, M. *Magic, its Rites and History*. Rider, London, 1960.

Eliade, M. *The Two and the One*. Harvill, London, 1966.

Grant, R.M. *Gnosticism*. Collins, London, 1960.

Hall, M.P. *The Most Holy Trinosophia of the Comte de St. Germain*. Philosophers Press, Los Angeles, 1949.

Jung, C.G. *Mysterium Coniunctionis*. Bollingen, New York, 1970.

_____ *Psychology and Alchemy*. Routledge and Kegan Paul, London, 1953.

Legge, F. *Forerunners and Rivals of Christianity*. University Books, New York, 1964.

Mead, G.R.S. *Fragments of a Faith Forgotten*. University Books, New York,

1960.

_____ *Pistis Sophia*. Watkins, London, 1921.

_____ *Thrice Greatest Hermes*. Theosophical Publishing Society, London and Benares, 1906.

Regardie, I. *The Philosopher's Stone*. Rider, London.

Trismosin, S. *Splendor Solis*. Kegan Paul, Trench and Trubner, London.

Waite, A.E. *The Brotherhood of the Rose Cross*. University Books, New York, 1961.

_____ *The Hermetic and Alchemical Works of Paracelsus*. University Books, New York, 1966.

_____ *The Works of Thomas Vaughan*. University Books, New York, 1969.

III

Bardon, F. *Initiation into Hermetics*. Osiris-Verlag, West Germany, 1962.

Butler, W. E. *The Magician*. Aquarian Press, London, 1963.

_____ *Magic, its Ritual Power and Purpose*. Aquarian Press, London, 1952.

Case, P. *The Tarot*. Macoy Publishing Co., New York, 1949.

Crowley, A. *Book Four* (Parts I and II). Wieland and Co., London, *c.* 1911-12.

_____ *Book of Thoth*. Weiser, New York, 1970.

_____ *Equinox*. Vol. I, Nos. i-x. Simkin, Marshall, Hamilton, Kent and Co., and Wieland and Co., London, 1909-13.

_____ *Magick in Theory and Practice*. Castle, New York, n.d.

Fortune, D. *The Mystical Qabalah*. Benn, London, 1962.

Franck, A. *The Kabbalah*. University Books, New York, 1969.

Fuller, J.F.C. *The Secret Wisdom of the Qabalah*. Rider, London.

Knight, G. *A Practical Guide to Qabalistic Symbolism* (2 vols.). Helios, Glos., 1965.

Mathers, S.L.M. *The Kabbalah Unveiled*. Routledge, Kegan Paul and Co.,

London, 1957.

Meyer, I. *Qabbalah*. Vincent Stuart and John M. Watkins, London, 1970.

Regardie, I. *The Golden Dawn* (4 vols.). The Aries Press, Chicago, 1938-1940.

____ *The Middle Pillar*. Llewellyn, Minnesota, 1970.

____ *The Tree of Life*. Rider, London, 1932.

Scholem, G. *Zohar*. Schocken Books, New York, 1970.

Sperling, H. and Simon, M. *The Zohar* (Vols. 1-5). The Soncino Press, London, 1970.

Stirling, J. *The Canon*. Elkin Mathews, London, 1899.

Symonds, J. *The Great Beast*. Rider, London, 1952.

____ *The Magic of Aleister Crowley*. Muller, London, 1958.

Waite, A.E. *The Holy Kabbalah*. University Books, New York, 1960.

Westcott, W. W. *The Study of the Kabalah*. Wehman Bros., New Jersey.

SECTION II: *The World of Shadows*

I

Grant, S. and K. *Austin Osman Spare*. Carfax Monograph IV. Privately printed, 1961.

Spare, A.O. *Earth: Inferno*. London, 1905; reprinted Askin, London, 1976.

____ *The Book of Pleasure (Self-Love)*. London, 1913.

____ *The Focus of Life*. London, 1921; reprinted Askin, London, 1976.

Spare, A.O. and Bax, C. *The Golden Hind*. Quarterly magazine (Vols. 1-8). Chapman and Hall, London, October 1922 – July 1924.

II

Cavendish, R. *The Black Arts*. Pan Books, London, 1967.

Garrison, O. *Tantra*. Julian Press, New York, 1964.

Hughes, P. *Witchcraft*. Penguin Books, Middlesex, 1970.

III

Budge, W. *Egyptian Magic*. University Books, New York, 1958.

Castaneda, C. *The Teachings of Don Juan*. Penguin Books, Middlesex, 1970.

Middleton, J. *Magic, Witchcraft and Curing*. Natural History Press, New York, 1967.

Sprenger, J. and Kramer, H. *Malleus Maleficarum*. Folio Society, London, 1968.

SECTION III: *The World of Dreams*

I

Books containing some of the best work by the 'Decadent' illustrators:

Harry Clarke: Poe's *Tales of Mystery and Imagination*. Harrap, London, 1919.

Goethe's *Faust*. Harrap, London, 1925.

Swinburne's *Selected Poems*. John Lane, London. 1928.

Coleridge's *The Ancient Mariner*. Maunsel and Co., *c.* 1913.

Alastair: *Fifty Drawings by Alastair*. Knopf, New York, 1925.

Wilde's *The Sphinx*. John Lane, London, 1920.

John Austen: *The Golden Hind*. Quarterly magazine. Vol. 2, No. 5. London, October 1923.

Books on the subject:

Richardson, D. *John Austen and the Inseparables*. William Jackson, London, 1930.

Salaman, M.C. *Modern Book Illustrators and their Work*. The Studio, London, 1914.

Taylor, J.R. *The Art Nouveau Book in Britain*. Methuen, London, 1966.

Books containing the best work by the Fairy Tale illustrators:

Edmund Dulac: Shakespeare's *The Tempest*. Hodder and Stoughton, London, *c.* 1913.

Rubaiyat of Omar Khayyam. Hodder and Stoughton, London, *c.* 1909.

Arthur Rackham: Irving's *Rip van Winkle*. Heinemann, London, 1905.

Wagner's *The Rhinegold and the Valkyrie*. Heinemann, London, 1910.

Kay Nielsen: *Andersen's Fairy Tales*. Hodder and Stoughton, London, 1924.

II

Alexandrian, S. *Surrealist Art*. Thames and Hudson, London, 1970.

Jean, M. *A History of Surrealist Painting*. Weidenfeld and Nicolson, London, 1967.

Nadeau, M. *A History of Surrealism*. Jonathan Cape, London, 1968.

Russell, J. *Max Ernst*. Thames and Hudson, London, 1967.

Soby, J. T. *Magritte*. The Museum of Modern Art, New York, 1965.

_____ *Yves Tanguy*. The Museum of Modern Art, New York, 1955.

Waldberg, P. *Surrealism*. Thames and Hudson, London, 1965.

III

Bardon, F. *Initiation into Hermetics*. Osiris-Verlag, West Germany, 1962.

Battersby, H. P. *Man Outside Himself*. University Books, New York, 1969.

Butler, W. E. *The Magician*. Aquarian Books, London, 1963.

Evans-Wentz, W.Y. *The Tibetan Book of the Dead*. Oxford University Press, 1927.

Muldoon, S. and Carrington, H. *The Projection of the Astral Body*. Rider, London, 1963.

Regardie, I. *The Middle Pillar*. Llewellyn, Minnesota, 1970.

SECTION IV: *The Search for Abraxas*

Hesse, H. *Demian*. Panther Books, London, 1969.

Johnson, R. *The Watcher on the Hills*. Hodder and Stoughton, London, 1959.

Laing, R.D. *The Politics of Experience and The Bird of Paradise*. Penguin, London, 1971.

Leary, T. *The Politics of Ecstasy*. Paladin, London, 1970.

Leary, T. *et al*. *The Psychedelic Experience*. University Books, New York, 1964.

INDEX